How
Successful
Schools
Work

SAGE has been part of the global academic community since 1965, supporting high quality research and learning that transforms society and our understanding of individuals, groups and cultures. SAGE is the independent, innovative, natural home for authors, editors and societies who share our commitment and passion for the social sciences.

Find out more at: **www.sagepublications.com**

How Successful Schools Work

Rona Tutt & Paul Williams

The Association for all School Leaders

Los Angeles | London | New Delhi
Singapore | Washington DC

SAGE Publications Ltd
1 Oliver's Yard
55 City Road
London EC1Y 1SP

SAGE Publications Inc.
2455 Teller Road
Thousand Oaks, California 91320

SAGE Publications India Pvt Ltd
B 1/I 1 Mohan Cooperative Industrial Area
Mathura Road
New Delhi 110 044

SAGE Publications Asia-Pacific Pte Ltd
3 Church Street
#10-04 Samsung Hub
Singapore 049483

Library of Congress Control Number: 2011938954

British Library Cataloguing in Publication data

A catalogue record for this book is available from the British Library

ISBN 978-1-4462-0769-7
ISBN 978-1-4462-0770-3 (pbk)

Typeset by C&M Digitals (P) Ltd, Chennai, India
Printed in India at Replika Press Pvt Ltd
Printed on paper from sustainable resources

Dedication

This book is dedicated to current and aspiring school leaders who have the vision, the resilience and the passion to lead the schools of today and tomorrow.

Contents

About the authors

Dr Rona Tutt OBE has taught pupils of all ages in state and independent, day and residential, mainstream and special schools. She is a former head teacher and has been a winner of the Leadership in Teaching Award. She has received an OBE for her services to special needs education. A Past President of the National Association of Head Teachers (NAHT), she continues to be involved with them as an SEN consultant.

Rona was on the Expert Group for the *Salt Review* (2009/10; DCSF, 2010) and the Project Steering Board for the *Complex Learning Difficulties and Disabilities Research Project* (2009–11). She writes regularly on a number of educational issues and, in 2011, she helped to create an online neuroscience module for the TDA. She is much in demand as a speaker. She spoke at the International Special and Inclusive Education Congress (ISEC 2010) in Belfast and, later that year, spoke at an education conference in Kuala Lumpur, as well as at various conferences throughout the UK.

Rona is the author of *Every Child Included* (2007); she co-authored *Educating Children with Complex Conditions: Understanding overlapping and co-existing developmental disorders* (with Dittrich, 2008) and wrote *Partnership Working to Support Special Educational Needs and Disabilities* in 2010. She has an MA in Linguistics and a PhD in the education of children with autism.

Paul Williams was born in Newcastle upon Tyne, but has been resident in London since becoming a teacher in 1973, working in Inner London comprehensive schools until 1987. He was an advisory teacher with ILEA until 1989, after which he was a deputy head until 1992. Since then, he has been head teacher at two London special schools – most recently in Harrow, which is also a specialist school.

Currently, Paul is a virtual head teacher for Looked After Children, and he has also been a School Improvement Partner. He is a member of The Schools Network (formerly SSAT) London Head Teacher Steering Group and was the London special school consultant head teacher for SSAT from 2008 to 2010. Paul has been a member of NAHT's National Executive since 2006 and a member of its Secondary Committee. He has chaired NAHT's SEND Committee since 2008.

Most recently, he has given evidence to Lord Bew's Review on Key Stage 2 Testing and Accountability. He has attended consultation meetings on the current National Curriculum Review, the Spending Review, changes to the Ofsted frameworks, the Achievement for All project and the Progression Guidance project. He has been involved with the joint SSAT/nasen/FLSE/NAHT SEND Green Paper launch and has made a presentation at the Westminster Education Forum.

Acknowledgements

We would like to offer our sincere thanks to all the schools, settings and services who allowed us to highlight their work and who gave generously of their time in talking to us and arranging our visits. They are:

Dr Penny Barratt	Head teacher, The Bridge School, Islington
Dame Yasmin Bevan	Executive principal, Denbigh High School and Challney High School for Boys and Community College, Luton
Rekha Bhakoo	Head teacher, Newton Farm School, Harrow
Anne Cockburn	Depute head teacher, Sanderson's Wynd Primary School, Tranent, Scotland
Mark Cole	Head teacher, Fawood Children's Centre, Brent
Colm Davis	Principal, Tor Bank School, Belfast
Jane Faint	Head teacher, St Teresa's RC School, Harrow
Kenny Fredrick	Head teacher, George Green's School, Tower Hamlets
Paul Green	Head teacher, Lyng Hall Specialist Sports College and Community College, Coventry
David Gregory	Head teacher, Fosse Way School, Radstock
Jack Hatch	Executive head teacher, St Bede's Academy, Bolton
Lesley James	Director of Business Development, RSA Academy, Tipton
Anne McCormick	Head teacher, Queens Park Academy, Bedford
Raymond McFeeters	Principal, Castle Tower School, Ballymena, NI
Andy McMorran	Principal, Ashfield Boys' High School, Belfast
Michael Newman	Principal, Victoria Primary School, Carrickfergus, NI
Helen Norris	Head of Specialist and Disability Services, Phoenix Children's Resource Centre, Bromley
Sue Painter	Head teacher, Portfield School, Haverfordwest, Wales
Jo Shuter	Head teacher, Quintin Kynaston School, Westminster
Tania Sidney-Roberts	Head teacher, Norwich Free School
Andrew Sleeth	Principal, Integrated College, Dungannon, NI
Jeff Smith	Head teacher, Anson Primary School, Brent
Sue Street	Director of e-learning, Harrow High School
Sue Tinson	Principal, Serendipity Centre, Southampton

Jan Wiggins	Head teacher, Bents Green School, Sheffield
Sue Winn	Head teacher, Southwater Infant Academy, Horsham
Fiona Waddell	Head teacher, Sanderson's Wynd Primary School, Tranent, Scotland

Thank you also to the following school leaders who contributed their thoughts and ideas:

Dave Bent

Tracey Capstick

Vicky Chatterjee

Viv Hinchliffe

Laura Lewis-Williams

June Roberts

Sarah Rostron

Gavin Sharp

Kerry Sternstein

Jill Williams

Matthew Williams

Caroline Woods

We are indebted to:

Professor Sonia Blandford, Chief Executive Officer, Achievement for All, for her help with the AfA material and case study.

Melanie Nind and Georgia Boorman of the University of Southampton for their research material on the Knowledge Transfer Partnership.

Toby Salt, Deputy Chief Executive and Toby Greany, Operational Director Research & Policy, National College for School Leadership, for their support and advice.

Sue Williamson, Chief Executive at The Schools Network (formerly SSAT).

Natalie Wood of the Future Leaders programme.

And, finally, to Dr Desmond Hamilton, for acting as chauffeur and driving us to our different destinations in Northern Ireland without a word of complaint.

Abbreviations and acronyms

ADHD	Attention deficit hyperactivity disorder
AEN	Additional educational needs
AET	Autism Education Trust
AfA	Achievement for All
AHT	Assistant head teacher
ASD	Autistic spectrum disorder
ASDAN	Award Scheme Development and Accreditation Network
BESD	Behavioural, emotional and social difficulties
BSF	Building Schools for the Future
BTEC	Business and Technology Council
CAMHS	Child and Adolescent Mental Health Service
CLDD	Complex learning difficulties and disabilities
CPD	Continuing professional development
DCS	Director of Children's Services
DST	Dyslexia–SpLD Trust
EBacc	English Baccalaureate
ECM	Every Child Matters
EHCP	Education, Health and Care Plan
ERA	Education Reform Act 1988
ESPP	Early Support Pilot Programme
EWS	Education Welfare Service
EYFS	Early Years Foundation Stage
FSM	Free school meals
G&T	Gifted and talented
GTP	Graduate Teacher Programme
IB	International Baccalaureate
IDP	Inclusion Development Programme
IPC	International Primary Curriculum
ITT	Initial teacher training
KTP	Knowledge Transfer Partnership
LLE	Local Leader of Education

MLE	Managed learning environment
NCSL	National College for School Leadership
NLE	National Leader of Education
NPQH	National Professional Qualification for Headship
NPQICL	National Professional Qualification in Integrated Centre Leadership
NQT	Newly qualified teacher
NSS	National Support School
LAC	Looked After Children
PCT	Primary Care Trust
PGCE	Post graduate certificate of education
PFI	Private finance initiative
PPP	Public–private partnership
PMLD	Profound and multiple learning difficulties
PRU	Pupil Referral Unit
QTS	Qualified teacher status
SLCN	Speech, language and communication needs
SEAL	Social and emotional aspects of learning
SEND	Special educational needs and disability
SLD	Severe learning difficulties
SLE	Specialist Leader of Education
SpLD	Specific learning difficulties
SLT	Senior leadership team
SMT	Senior management team
SSAT	Specialist Schools and Academies Trust (now The Schools Network)
STRB	School Teachers' Review Body
TDA	Training and Development Agency for Schools
UKRP	United Kingdom Resilience Programme
UTC	University Technical College
VLE	Virtual learning environment

How to use this book

This book shows how the role and style of school leadership is undergoing significant change and illuminates, through conversations with school leaders and case studies of schools across the UK, the way that innovative and inspirational school leaders enable schools to be successful.

The six main chapters include the following:

- a summary of what is covered in the chapter at the start
- 'Key points' highlighted where necessary
- 'Questions for reflection' and activities, which are given at relevant points to encourage the reader to interact with the text and to provide ideas for wider discussion and debate
- case studies of schools, settings and services, which are a main feature of each chapter and serve to illustrate the imaginative practice that exists
- photocopiable material, placed at the end of the relevant chapter
- suggestions for further reading and useful websites at the end of each chapter.

The chapters are arranged in the following order:

The Introduction sets the scene by explaining how the role of school leaders has changed in response to changing demands.

Chapter 1 gives reports of conversations with current and aspiring school leaders as well as case studies, in order to determine the reasons why teachers are attracted to school leadership roles.

Chapter 2 provides examples of different models and styles of leadership, and of how schools are changing their structures to accommodate new ways of working.

Chapter 3 looks at how school leaders strive to provide an inclusive environment and gives case studies of how this is achieved in four very different settings.

Chapter 4 discusses the power invested in school leaders and how this can be used to decide how to organise the school and the different ways the curriculum is delivered.

Chapter 5 concentrates on the importance of well-being, both for staff and pupils, and how the actions of school leaders and the environment they create impact on people.

Chapter 6 considers how innovative school leaders manage to stay at the forefront of events, in order to seize opportunities as they arise.

The Conclusion draws together some of the threads, in order to pull out the characteristics of innovative leaders who lead successful schools.

It was exhilarating to have the opportunity to talk to so many school leaders who, despite its pressures and stresses, were enthused by their role, and to visit so many very different settings in Northern Ireland, Scotland and Wales, as well as England. We hope that something of the flavour of the incredible work these leaders do (and all school leaders like them), with such insight and foresight, comes across through the pages of this book.

Introduction

Chapter overview

This chapter sets the scene for the rest of the book. It describes why the role of school leaders has gained such prominence and why the leaders of today need to be innovative as a major part of their role. It looks at how schools, in keeping with the rest of society, are going for flatter, less hierarchical structures.

To establish the context further, mention is made of some of the educational changes affecting how schools are led, which took place between the 1960s and the present day. It covers how schools are entering a period of having more autonomy, but at a time of severe financial constraints.

The last part of the chapter is concerned with the different roles that head teachers are fulfilling and the opportunities there are for the schools they lead to contribute to innovative leadership through collaboration with other schools and services.

The importance of school leadership

Since the late 1980s, schools have been undergoing a period of massive change, both in the sense of the diversity of schools that have been created and in terms of what is expected of schools and of school leaders. This has resulted in the quality of leadership being recognised as a key factor in a school's success. In 2000, the establishment by the government of a National College for School Leadership (NCSL) was a clear demonstration of the importance given to developing leadership capacity in schools. In November 2005, the School Teachers' Review Body (STRB) took up this theme in its 15th Report, when it recommended that there should be an independent study to examine the roles, responsibilities, structures and reward systems for school leaders in England and Wales. Subsequently, the DfES commissioned *The Independent Study of School Leadership* (PricewaterhouseCoopers, 2007), which said: 'Not only does leadership capacity dictate current performance, but it is a crucial factor in the readiness of organisations to face the future' (p. 1).

The Report found that in England and Wales the leadership of schools was generally of high quality and had been improving consistently since the mid-1990s. It suggested that the quality of teaching in the classroom was the biggest influence on pupils' learning, followed by the quality of leadership in the school. As it is often the head teacher and the leadership team who choose the staff, not only do they have influence through the way they carry out their role, but they are largely responsible for who is employed to teach in their school. So, in this respect, although school

1

leaders were placed second by the writers of the report, their influence has an effect on the quality of teaching through the appointments they make, as well as their own direct influence. The report also found that school leaders generally command widespread respect in society, where they are perceived as providing particularly good examples of leadership. More recently, an NCSL report published in 2009 referred to school leaders as belonging to 'a profession in transition' (2009a).

The pace and extent of the changes bombarding schools have meant that school leaders have needed to be prepared to be both forward-thinking and innovative. As each fresh opportunity has presented itself, they have had to weigh up which route to take and how to make sure their school remains at the cutting edge of developments in the curriculum, in technology and in the pedagogy arising from knowing more about how children learn. At the same time, there has been a growing concern for the well-being of children and young people, as they, too, have to cope with the effects of the accelerating pace of change, both inside and outside school. The case studies in this book demonstrate what has been achieved by leaders who have responded to change, by seeing it as a means of taking their schools forward and who have made sure that any alteration in the way the school operates will be of benefit to all the children and young people for whom they are responsible. These are leaders who are never satisfied with what they have already achieved, but who are always looking towards the next development. The hallmark of these leaders, regardless of their personality, is their energy, enthusiasm and entrepreneurship.

Training of head teachers

Although Headlamp and the Headteacher Induction Programme (HIP) had put in brief appearances to help train heads who were new in post, training teachers to become heads did not happen until 1997, when the National Professional Qualification for Headship (NPQH) was introduced. At first, this was an option for anyone seeking headship, but from April 2009, it became a mandatory qualification. In the autumn of 2010, the coalition government's White Paper *The Importance of Teaching* (DfE, 2010c) noted that there would be a further review, to make sure the NPQH was focusing on the key skills needed for headship in today's schools. This was followed by a DfE announcement in December 2011, that it would be seeking to make the qualification non-mandatory, although the revised NPQH would remain as a mark of quality for those seeking headship.

Head teachers and school leaders

At one time, head teachers were clearly identified as the leaders in their schools. They were expected to make the decisions, in conjunction with their governing bodies, who often took it as read that heads knew what they were doing and were content to follow their lead. As a result of schools being expected to take on more and more responsibilities, the concept of *school leaders*, rather than that of head teacher, gained credence. This fitted in with a general wish, both within and outside education, to have less hierarchical systems of leadership and management.

Traditionally, head teachers have been supported by deputy head teachers who are able to deputise for them when they are away from the school. In 2000, a new pay structure was introduced and the role of assistant head teacher was created. Heads, deputy heads and assistant heads were placed on a separate leadership scale. In this book, as well as talking about head teachers as the key player in the leadership team, recognition is given to the importance of the leadership team as a whole, and, indeed, to the role played by other staff.

As well as heads, deputies and assistant heads, many leadership teams have expanded to include non-teaching staff, such as school bursars, someone to represent the support staff such as a higher level teaching assistant (HLTA) and many other posts. There is no longer a blueprint for what a leadership team should look like and some of the case studies in the following chapters show how schools are adopting a structure that suits their particular establishment.

A historical perspective

In order to establish the context for the manner in which schools are diversifying and developing, it may be helpful to mention briefly some of the key points that have shaped the way that schools are beginning to look today. In the 1960s and 1970s, schools were left alone to organise themselves largely as they saw fit. This changed significantly with the 1988 Education Reform Act (ERA).

Before 1988

This is the time that is sometimes referred to as education's 'secret garden'. On the whole, head teachers trusted their staff and classroom doors were kept closed. At secondary level, the curriculum was partly determined by the syllabuses of public examinations, but at primary level, apart from pupils who were still sitting the 11+ exam to get into grammar schools, there were no such pressures. The Plowden Report (DES, 1967) had an enormous influence on primary education, as it suggested the need for a more child-centred view of education. Plowden also highlighted the need for head teachers to be trained for their role, although this did not happen until much later.

1988 and beyond

The Education Reform Act of 1988 introduced a national curriculum, testing at 7, 11 and 14, created the Local Management of Schools (LMS) and paved the way for Ofsted, which came into existence in 1992. Although the national curriculum was designed to cover the education of 5–16-year-olds, it was a secondary model that assumed children of all ages should be taught through separate subjects. Each group of subject experts working separately were determined that *their* subject should take up a large slab of teaching time, with the consequence that it was impossible to teach the whole of the national curriculum and it had to be scaled back.

Primary education

In 1992, three well-known figures in educational circles – Robin Alexander, Jim Rose and Chris Woodhead – tried to find a balance between Plowden's stance on primary education and the more traditional view taken by the national curriculum. They published *Curriculum Organisation and Classroom Practice in Primary Schools: A discussion paper* (DES, 1992), which came to be known as the report of the Three Wise Men. More recently, Rose and Alexander competed to produce a revised primary school curriculum. With a change of government in 2010, the whole of the curriculum is being looked at afresh (see Chapter 4).

ECM and the Children Act

As well as the ongoing debates about what should be taught in schools, the Labour government altered the face of the education service by bringing in a Green Paper, *Every Child Matters* (ECM), in 2003 (DfES, 2003), followed the next year by the Children Act (DfES, 2004a). Local authorities (LAs) were encouraged to bring together education and social care under a single director of children's services and to work more closely with health services.

Schools were asked to place themselves at the centre of their local communities by providing a range of services, being more accessible to the community and by opening for longer periods of time. Children's centres, some of them attached to schools, were established to provide education and childcare, as well as access to a range of services and activities in one place. Although the current government has been less focused on this agenda, all schools now offer a range of out-of-school activities to their pupils, to families and to the wider community.

A change of government

After Labour had been in power for 13 years, the general election in May 2010 saw a coalition government being formed by the Conservatives and the Liberal Democrats. Any hopes that this might mean a slowing down in the pace of change was short-lived, as the new government set about putting its stamp on education policy. The Academies Act (DfE, 2010a) was rushed through parliament before the first summer recess. A new, slimmed down national curriculum was promised. Several educational quangos (quasi-autonomous non-governmental organisations) were either scrapped or turned into executive agencies, and an extensive Education Bill started its progress through parliament in January 2011, becoming an Act by the end of that year.

Leadership and management

In 2005, regulations were put in place requiring head teachers to review their staffing structures by the end of 2008. Since then, it has been up to the head and the governing body to decide the structure that is right for them at any given time and to review this structure, at least annually, as the school's requirements change.

Some schools have both a senior leadership team (SLT), which focuses on the strategic direction of the school and a senior management team (SMT), where subject or key stage coordinators are responsible for leading subjects or departments. However, this distinction is sometimes blurred and schools may have only one team, or call the one that they have an SMT rather than an SLT.

Different roles for school leaders and schools

Today, headship takes many forms. There may, for instance, be two people sharing the role, or, alternatively, one head who takes on more than one school, either on a temporary or permanent basis.

Co-head teachers

Since the first example of co-headship occurred in the 1990s, several different models have emerged. These include job-share headships, where two people work part-time as part of a single head teacher post, and joint headship, where both head teachers work full-time and share responsibility for the leadership of the school. At a time of concern about the number of people coming forward for headships, governing bodies may decide to consider job-share applicants in order to enlarge the pool of applicants.

Chief executives and executive head teachers

Chief executives and executive heads are often associated with federations of schools, although federated schools do not necessarily have executive heads, and schools that have executive heads are not necessarily in a federation. The Education Act of 2002 (DfES, 2002) allowed the creation of a single governing body across two or more maintained schools. This is one type of federation, but schools can also decide to federate while keeping their own heads and governing bodies. Executive headship is also used to enable an outstanding school to be paired with one that needs to develop its systems, structures and expertise.

Other titles in use

These include: Advisory Head for experienced heads who are used by the LA to support other heads; Associate Heads who might, for instance, work alongside an Acting Head Teacher; Acting or Interim Heads who fill in before a permanent head is appointed; and 'Virtual Head Teachers' who support the designated teachers for Looked After Children (LAC).

Additional roles alongside headship

As well as the different types of headships referred to previously, head teachers may take on a number of additional roles alongside their post as substantive head.

Local Leaders of Education (LLEs)

Most LAs have joined the Local Leaders of Education (LLEs) programme, whereby successful head teachers in a locality, work with one or more other heads to support them in building their capacity for sustained improvement.

National Leaders of Education (NLEs) and National Support Schools

When a head is appointed as an NLE, the school becomes a national support school, meaning that other members of the leadership team, as well as the head, will be involved in supporting other schools.

In the White Paper *The Importance of Teaching* (DfE, 2010c), referred to earlier, the government expressed its intention of doubling the number of LLEs and NLEs and introducing a new category of Specialist Leaders of Education (SLEs). Unlike LLEs and NLEs, these will be excellent teachers, who occupy positions of leadership below that of head teacher. Although all these schemes are run by the NCSL, SLEs may be linked to teaching schools once both have become more established. (There is more about teaching schools in Chapter 6.)

Preparing for headship

Partly in response to a growing concern about a shortage of teachers coming forward for headship, new routes into headship have been developed.

Accelerate to Headship

Accelerate to Headship has two routes: Future Leaders and Tomorrow's Heads. Both programmes are concerned with developing the next generation of school leaders and offer accelerated leadership development. The first sets out a programme for achieving headship within five years, including completing the NPQH in the final year, while the second route enables those who have set their sights on headship to continue working in their current schools, while being supported in developing their leadership skills by an adviser.

Throughout this book, there are case studies of school leaders who carry out many of the roles that have been mentioned in this Introduction. The next chapter has reports of conversations as well as case studies, which illustrate what it was that attracted people to become school leaders at a time of significant change and challenge.

Further reading

Alexander, R. (ed.) (2009) *Children, their World, their Education: Final report and recommendations of the Cambridge Primary Review*. London: Routledge.

Department for Education (DfE) (2010c) *The Importance of Teaching*. Available at: www.tsoshop.co.uk

National College for School Leadership (NCSL) (2009a) *School Leadership Today*. Nottingham: NCSL.

PricewaterhouseCoopers (2007) *Independent Study into School Leadership*. Available at: www.teachernet.gov.uk/publications

1

The attraction of leadership

> **Chapter overview**
>
> This chapter explores what attracts people to the idea of becoming school leaders. This is pursued through reports of conversations with teachers at different stages of their career, including aspiring leaders and those who are already assistant head teachers or deputy head teachers.
>
> In addition, the views are given of those who have attained headship and who are taking on fresh challenges, either in terms of improving their own school, or by taking on additional responsibilities.
>
> In addition to the case studies, the chapter concludes with a mention of the newest type of academy, namely the free school.

The changing nature of school leadership

There is no doubt that demands on head teachers have increased steadily over the last two decades and the job itself has changed out of all recognition. Rising expectations of what schools will achieve, combined with the amount of bureaucracy and accountability involved, have made many teachers think twice about moving up the career ladder.

A group of head teachers who were discussing these changes recently, commented on how they had affected long-standing and newer heads differently, with those who were coming into the role knowing what they were taking on, while established heads have had to adjust to a way of life where change not only happens all the time, but occurs at an ever quicker pace. Despite the workload and the pressures, however, there are heads who not only take on the role, but who actively seek additional challenges.

Challenges and opportunities

Throughout this book, there are accounts of school leaders who have been proactive, and who never stop finding new ways of driving their schools forward, despite the sometimes overwhelming demands of the job.

Assistant and deputy head teachers

As mentioned in the previous chapter, the role of assistant head was introduced in September 2000, as part of a reorganisation of school leadership posts. As new staffing structures came into place, both primary and secondary schools were keen to appoint assistant head teachers. Between 2005 and 2009, assistant heads in primary schools doubled in number, while those in secondary schools increased by 21 per cent. At the same time, numbers of deputy heads decreased by 7 per cent, which was a cause of some concern, as it was felt that there might be fewer teachers ready to take up headships. However, there are plenty of examples of teachers moving on to headship without being deputies first.

The attraction of leading a school

In the following paragraphs, there are accounts of teachers who are aspiring heads and of assistant head teachers and deputy head teachers who explain the reasons why they took on their current role. Some are aiming for headship and some prefer to remain in their current role.

Aspiring heads

The Accelerate to Headship programmes, mentioned in the previous chapter, have proved to be an important route in trying to get more teachers interested in headship at a time when there is a bulge in the numbers due to retire. Two of the many teachers who have followed this route are now assistant heads in London. Both have followed the Future Leaders programme, but one took a more circuitous route by beginning the Teach First programme. (Teach First fast tracks promising graduates and places them in the classroom after six weeks of intensive training. They then spend two years in tough secondary schools.)

The first graduate had always wanted to teach, but after starting the Teach First programme, she was not sure that she had made the right decision and so she worked in the city for three years. She said that this confirmed to her that teaching was the right profession for her after all. Hearing about Future Leaders, she joined the programme and she is now working as an assistant head in a challenging secondary school in London. She intends to become a deputy and then a head and would want to stay in a similar type of school. One of her current projects is to evaluate the Opening Minds approach (which is featured in Chapter 4).

The second Future Leaders' entrant to the profession is a young man who never planned to be a teacher. However, after leaving university, he decided to take a post graduate certificate of education (PGCE) course in a shortage subject. After teaching for six years in two different schools, and having come across what he describes as some inspirational head teachers, he began applying for assistant head teacher posts. When he was not immediately successful, he decided to apply for the Future Leaders programme.

As part of his training, he went to Chicago, where he visited a range of charter schools and met some outstanding leaders. He took away from the experience the feeling that he would want to have a school that ensured students who were at risk of failure could have interventions very early. It also reinforced his view that relationships between teachers and students are at the heart of a successful school. He comments:

> Future Leaders has given me a range of skills to become a successful head teacher but most importantly, they have created a network of support for those days when things are tough and advice and support are needed.

Other routes to headship

Fifteen years ago, when looking for employment, a young lady with no experience of helping in school, took on a job as a temporary teaching assistant in a special school. She enjoyed the work and obtained a permanent post in the same school. Later, she decided to train as a teacher. As she already had a degree, she was able to get a place on the Graduate Teacher Programme (GTP). Some years later, she became the key stage 3 coordinator and joined the senior leadership team (SLT). Although she is not an assistant head, she continues to plan for the next stage of her career, encouraged by her head who recognises her potential. She believes that headship would enable her to take responsibility for the well-being of staff, while having additional scope to put forward her own ideas for the school's development. She sees this, not so much as a career plan, but as part of her life plan, as she has tried all along to balance the needs of her family with what is right for her own development.

Assistant heads

In one large primary school, as well as a deputy head, there are three assistant heads, who are given considerable responsibilities and scope for their own professional development.

One assistant head is an early years specialist, who, before taking on her current role, had always believed she would aim to be head of a nursery school or children's centre, or an early years adviser. However, since taking on a wider role, including that of being the school's SENCo, her interests and options have broadened, so she is not sure which direction she will take, but she remains keen to further her career.

A second assistant head has always been very ambitious and more or less assumed that headship would be her aim. However, having recently had her first child, she is more conscious of the workload attached to being a head and the impact this might have on family life. At present, she is thinking in terms of taking up a deputy head's post in a smaller primary school. In the longer term, she is still interested in becoming a head, but it would have to be at a time that was right for the family.

The third assistant head has also had a baby recently and is currently on maternity leave. Some time ago, she completed a Middle Managers' course, which she found very valuable, particularly as it gave her an opportunity to meet other people in similar positions. At the time, she considered moving on to the National Professional Qualification for Headship (NPQH) quite quickly. Although she is still aiming for headship, she was concerned that the expectation that people would aim for headship within a specified timescale may have put off some teachers from applying to take the NPQH, and she is pleased this restriction has been lifted.

Deputy heads

By way of contrast to the three assistant heads, the next two people are already deputy heads and see it as a long-term role in its own right. They have both been in the position for over 10 years, one in a secondary special school and one in a large primary school. Their satisfaction with their present roles may be partly because they have been given plenty of scope to use and develop their talents where they are now, and are left to run their schools on a regular basis. And this is, perhaps, an indication of how the role is changing. So many heads now take on additional roles or responsibilities that they need to be able to rely on an experienced deputy to be in charge of the school while they are engaged in their wider role.

The special school deputy enjoys being involved in professional development and, if she were to change her current position, would be more likely to find a role in the field of professional development than in seeking a headship. She feels she already has plenty of opportunity to try out new ideas and suggests that headship could be more restricting than her current post. The other deputy head works in a primary school that has expanded considerably and so her responsibilities have increased while she has remained in the same post. As the head has many roles, including being a National Leader of Education (NLE), she enjoys being in the driving seat and feels no urge to be the person who is ultimately responsible for the whole school. Both these deputies are very active school leaders, without wanting to become head teachers.

The final deputy teaches in a primary school in Northern Ireland, where he is known as a deputy principal. Some years ago, he took a Middle Managers' course, which he found both helpful and enjoyable. He followed this by taking the Professional Qualification for Headship (PQH), which is the equivalent of the NPQH in Northern Ireland. Despite finding the training useful, he believes his real training for headship has resulted from being in charge of his school for a year as acting principal.

Other school leaders

Although assistant and deputy headship are the more traditional routes to becoming a head teacher, with the diversification of leadership teams in schools, there are other pathways emerging. An example of this is Sue Street, who is currently director of e-learning at a high school in London.

Case study: Sue Street

Sue's rather unusual journey towards school leadership in England started 15 years ago in New Zealand, where she trained first as a doctor and then as an educational administrator. However, she realised belatedly that what she really wanted to do was to teach. After working in a school in her home country, she came to teach in England, originally for one year, but then decided she would like to stay here.

She worked in several schools in London before becoming a local authority adviser, where she gained experience of working with schools in difficult circumstances. She found that she relished a role that combined trouble shooting and problem solving with the opportunity to become an advocate for the professional development of all staff. This led to Sue being asked to take on a succession of management roles.

Last year, Sue completed the NPQH as she very much wants to become a head teacher. She has a clear idea about why she would like the role and what she would want to achieve. She sums this up as: putting teaching and learning at the heart of what the school does; seeing the professional development of staff as central to a school's ability to move forward; and improving the achievement of all pupils. Sue has been in schools where the head has not stayed long enough to make an impact and she says she would hope to remain in her first headship for at least five years.

 Questions for reflection

1 Do you think every school should have a deputy head and what are your reasons?
2 What do you see as the balance of responsibilities between assistant heads and deputy heads?
3 Should the role of deputy head be seen as a valuable one in its own right or only as a stepping stone to becoming a head?
4 List some of the advantages and disadvantages of becoming a head teacher in today's climate.

Managing change

Much has been written about the management of change and the need for school leaders to take staff with them in effecting change within a school. Michael Fullan began identifying change as an important theme in the early 1980s and has followed this through in his more recent writings, such as in his book *Leading in a Culture of Change* (2001), where he continues to stress the need for leaders to understand the process of change.

Some changes are forced on schools by events at national or local level. Others are changes that come about because a school, setting or service wishes to move forward in a particular way. If the latter, then it is easier to control the process, but it is still necessary to realise how people are affected by, and respond to, change. Throughout this book, there are examples of school leaders who have managed significant changes, sometimes in response to changing circumstances and sometimes to bring about the change they wanted to see. How they handled those changes helps to demonstrate the way they lead.

Managing change within the same school

In the past, it was not particularly unusual to find teachers who were not necessarily aiming to become heads, but who, when a particular opportunity arose, decided to take it. In recent years, this approach has been less likely to work, as a decision had to be made as to whether or not to take the NPQH. The next case study involves a head teacher of a Catholic primary and nursery school, who has devoted her energies to seeing through changes within her own school rather than feeling the urge to move elsewhere.

 Case study: Jane Faint

Jane took her first job as a class teacher in her present school, before later becoming the deputy head. Even then, she did not really consider headship, as she found the deputy's role sufficiently fulfilling. However, when the headship became vacant in her own school, she decided to apply, because she felt she was in a position to know how best to move the school forward.

During her time at the school, it has expanded from one- to two-form entry, with 468 pupils aged 3–11. It has had several refurbishments and extensions and these alterations, together with the change in the pupil population, has made it seem almost like running two different schools. To start with, the children were mainly White British, but now the second largest group are Black African pupils and 32 different languages are spoken. Because of the changing needs of the children, Jane has adjusted the curriculum from an emphasis on numeracy to concentrating on developing literacy.

When numeracy was the biggest issue, Jane started to run a maths surgery, so that any child in Year 6 could come to her for help. Now, other teachers have taken a similar approach for children wanting help with literacy. While there is more intensive intervention for pupils who need it, these surgeries are an imaginative way of ironing out smaller problems that arise.

Jane has employed the same practical approach to making sure every child feels included. When the school found it had a number of hearing impaired children, staff and children developed their signing skills. Similarly, when the first child using a wheelchair arrived, Jane took outside advice to ensure the pupil could be fully included in PE and Games lessons.

Jane says that 'the biggest challenge is to meet the constantly changing picture of what is expected of schools and balancing this with the needs of the children'. She knows that staff have to work that much harder to maintain standards.

Managing a change of status

The Academies Act (DfE, 2010a) saw a switch from 'failing' schools reopening as academies, to encouraging outstanding schools to take on this new status. The next case study is of an infant school head teacher in West Sussex, whose school was one of the first to become an academy for this age group.

 Case study: Sue Winn

The school is a large, three-form entry infant school with 270 pupils. On the same site, there is a private nursery and a new junior academy. The infant and junior schools work closely together and are fund-raising jointly. A swimming pool was top of the pupils' recent wish list, together with a Pets Corner!

The children at the infant school are used to having their voices heard. The school council used the school's Self-Evaluation Form (SEF) and adapted eight questions from it to create a Children's SEF. The next step is going to be to use this as the basis for a Children's School Development Plan (SDP), which will become part of the school's SDP.

When asked why she wanted her school to become an academy, Sue gave the following reasons:

- more control over funding at a time of financial cutbacks
- greater ability to purchase services required without the budget being top sliced by the local authority
- greater freedom to make decisions.

As examples of the greater freedom she feels she enjoys, Sue quoted being able to knock down a wall in order to create more space without having to wait for permission, and arranging a 'Lunch on Wheels' service, rather than having to make hot meals on the premises.

Sue says: 'Stripping back bureaucracy and focusing on how to improve provision further is what it is about.'

The previous two examples were of heads who, in different ways, effected change while staying in the same school. The final case study in this chapter is of a special school head teacher who moved from East Anglia to South Yorkshire because she was drawn to the challenge of creating a new special school with a range of features that interested her.

Establishing a new school

Jan Wiggins was appointed in April 2011, before the school opened in the September of that year as a secondary school for pupils on the autism spectrum.

Case study: Jan Wiggins

Jan is another head who enjoys a challenge, so when she saw an opportunity to open a new school in Sheffield, she jumped at the chance. The school is part of Sheffield's reorganisation of its special schools to create nine new or refurbished schools, all of which will work very closely with mainstream schools.

Jan was appointed before the school opened, so that she would have time to plan for a school taking 162 pupils aged 11–19, with a diagnosis of autism. The school will be open for 52 weeks a year. Jan will head a multi-agency team who will be able to support the students' health, therapy and care needs. Jan says that what interested her could be summed up as the opportunity to:

- establish a 52-week residential provision
- provide an extended day with respite provision
- run an outreach team to offer advice to other schools and to support transition arrangements.

Jan says that the lure of a new school building with the facilities these children need on one site and the opportunity to lead a multi-professional staff team, made her decide that this was the right move for her.

Heads taking on additional roles

As mentioned in the opening chapter, the government is keen to increase the number of Local Leaders in Education (LLEs) and National Leaders of Education (NLEs). Rekha Bhakoo is head of a primary school in London. As she is an NLE, her school is a National Support School (NSS). She says she enjoys the challenge of supporting other schools and finds that most schools welcome the contact with someone from outside the school. With some, it can take longer to establish a relationship. So far, Rekha has worked with schools in her own local authority but she is now being asked to work further afield as well.

The rest of her leadership team, including the deputy head and bursar, are already involved in working with other schools, and so she is delighted that their contribution can be recognised in future, not just through being part of an NSS, but by being seen as Specialist Leaders of Education (SLEs). Rekha feels that this will give them proper recognition for the work that they do beyond her school. She is committed to the idea that, with the pace of change in education, leaders need to stay ahead of the game. She says: 'To develop you have to be innovative and to think outside the box, not just for today and tomorrow, but for the next five years.'

Writing for the NCSL, David Hargreaves (2010) suggested that leaders of outstanding schools fall into two categories: those who want to work with other schools, and those who do not have an interest in system leadership. (System leadership is described more fully in the next chapter.) For the former, it is this extra dimension to their work that maintains their interest in headship.

Free schools: a new type of challenge

As well as all the opportunities open to heads and their leadership teams, an entirely different kind of option has now arrived. This is the advent of the academies known as *free schools*, the first tranche of which opened in September 2011.

While development of the academies has not been without controversy, free schools have attracted even more concerns about who will be running them, how accountable they will be, and their impact on the schools around them. When the government invited groups to apply to set up a free school, there were 323 applications, with 24 having opened in September 2011: 17 primary schools, five secondary schools and two all-age schools.

One of the first to open was the Norwich Free School, where Tania Sidney-Roberts is the founder and principal. She has 20 years' teaching experience behind her, has been a deputy head and holds the NPQH. Tania always wanted to run her own school. As soon as she knew she was in with a chance of being in the first tranche of free schools, she gathered together a group that included a solicitor and a building consultant, as well as people with expertise in the fields of finance, ICT and PR. This has helped her to form a Board of Governors with committees for: Premises, Finance, Curriculum, Personnel, Admissions and PR. The governing body also includes local councillors from the main political parties.

Tania says she had no difficulty in attracting enough pupils or appointing staff. The school will be open for 51 weeks a year and will include a child-care facility. Although she describes the last year as very hard work, she says she has enjoyed the process and the school was ready to open as planned in September 2011.

〰〰 Questions for reflection

1 Do you agree with the move to allow (i) primary schools and (ii) special schools and PRUs to become academies?
2 What do you see as the advantages and disadvantages of becoming an academy?
3 If the present trend of having more academies continues, what do you think the impact will be on local authorities?
4 How do you feel about free schools? What might prove to be their strengths and weaknesses?

Although it is too early to judge the effects of having an increasing proportion of schools breaking away from LA control, as most schools want to work collaboratively, it is to be hoped that partnership working will continue to flourish. In his analysis, *Achieving More Together: Adding value through partnership* (2008), Robert Hill is clear that partnerships are the way to enable the school system to continue to improve.

While some teachers may be put off by the size and complexity of the modern school leader's role, others are attracted to leadership because of the chance to put into practice their ideas on how to enhance teaching and learning, and to support staff in developing the skills they need to work in an ever-changing and increasingly complex environment.

Further reading

Fullan, M. (2001) *Leading in a Culture of Change.* San Francisco, CA: Jossey-Bass.

Hargreaves, D. (2010) *Creating a Self-improving School System.* Nottingham: NCSL.

Hill, R. (2008) *Achieving More Together: Adding value through partnership.* Leicester: ASCL.

Tutt, R. (2010) *Partnership Working to Support Children with Special Educational Needs and Disabilities.* London: Sage.

2

Changing styles of leadership

Chapter overview

This chapter considers how the style of leadership has changed from a hierarchical pattern to one that sees the importance of leadership being distributed across a range of staff. It looks at how school leaders are managing an expanded role and a wider workforce.

Some of these roles have been created to meet the needs of a more complex pupil population, as well as a more personalised approach to all students' learning, while others have been created to recognise the advantages of respecting the importance of relationships with pupils, their families and communities.

The chapter includes case studies of what this has meant in terms of the leadership styles that have been adopted and how far school leaders have adjusted their styles to the situations in which they find themselves.

The current situation

In the 2009 review of school leadership by the National College for School Leadership (NCSL), mentioned in the introductory chapter, it was noted that leadership is being distributed across diverse teams, with school leaders often working beyond their own organisations. The NCSL had concerns that fewer teachers were interested in becoming heads because of the increasing stresses of the job, the time commitment making it difficult to maintain a sensible work–life balance, and the risks involved.

The element of risk does not lie so much in the risks that school leaders choose to take, but in the fact that job security has all but disappeared. There is always the threat of allegations being made, and even though the vast majority turn out to be unsubstantiated, they can still damage a teacher's career. There is concern about the emphasis placed on raw data, with schools being held accountable by Ofsted and the local authority (LA) for any dip in test and exam results, when it is clearly unrealistic to assume that it is possible to raise standards year on year and when many of the factors contributing to how children perform are beyond the school's control.

Despite this, as the previous chapter has indicted, there are teachers who are keen to become heads, as well as heads who are responsive to taking on wider roles. In this chapter, the emphasis is on how leadership styles have changed in order to accommodate new ways of working, increased expectations of what schools will deliver and the continuous drive for school improvement. Indeed, it is recognised by many that the emphasis on school improvement that originated in the 1980s, has led to a higher quality of school leader and that this can be traced back to the amount of collaboration that has become common among schools, despite successive governments encouraging competition through the publication of 'league tables'. Although training and additional qualifications have an important place, it has become increasingly apparent that schools and school leaders learn most from each other. This is confirmed by David Hargreaves (2010). He sees schools working together and system leadership (heads working across schools) as the route to a self-improving system. Although competition between schools has not been eliminated, the coalition government's desire to give more freedom and autonomy to individual schools is combined with a notion that schools, whether academies or community schools, should not be working in isolation.

Leadership, management and administration

School leadership is a comparatively recent topic for discussion, debate and research and is allied to and interlocks with school management and school administration. Indeed, sometimes the terms are used almost interchangeably. Leadership is generally seen as being strategic, with effective school leaders often described as being inspirational or visionary. Management, on the other hand, is more concerned with the operational level of running an organisation such as a school. Administration refers to the backroom work that must be done to support the smooth running of the establishment. An illustration of how these terms are interrelated becomes apparent when thinking in terms of the role of a school's governing body.

Governors are often reminded that their role is strategic and that they should not become too involved with the day-to-day running of the school, but leave that to the head and his or her staff. However, when looked at from the head teacher's perspective, the head and the leadership team will be seen as working at a strategic level as well as managing the school on a daily basis.

Some schools differentiate between a senior leadership team (SLT) and a Senior Management Team (SMT), while others may not specifically name two teams, but will have heads of department or key stage coordinators who will take responsibility for the day-to-day running of their departments. In practical terms, leadership and management are often put together (as in Ofsted reports) because, in terms of school leadership, it may not make much sense to separate them.

As already stated, 'leadership' as a theoretical concept attracted little attention until the 1990s when Tony Bush, amongst others, became interested in adapting some of the ideas on leadership in a wider context. In the fourth edition of his book on *Theories of Educational Leadership and Management* (2011), Bush lists six management models and 10 leadership models. The first of the leadership models he calls a managerial model, again demonstrating the closeness of the two concepts. Until relatively recently, there has been a fascination with *leaders* rather than leader*ship* and there has been a tendency to focus on school leaders, and particularly on head teachers, and to portray the best of them as being charismatic or having outstanding personalities. Now, however, the focus has shifted more to a consideration of the nature of leadership itself.

Models of school leadership

It is apparent that successful head teachers use a variety of structures and systems as a way of organising their schools. The list below details some of the models that have been suggested and which are not necessarily mutually exclusive:

1　Transformational leadership was the dominant model in the 1990s. It moved into education from other settings, and centres on the head teacher being the one to articulate a vision and ensure it is implemented.
2　Post-transformational leadership moved on from this to seeing others as well as the head being involved in establishing a vision for the school.
3　Distributed leadership is the idea of leadership being spread across a team rather than residing in a single leader, with staff influencing how a school develops and taking collective responsibility for its progress.
4　System leadership does not replace the idea of leadership being distributive, but adds a new dimension, as it refers to heads leading or supporting other institutions.
5　Sustainable leadership is another term that has come in alongside distributed leadership. It emphasises the need for succession planning (which is mentioned again in Chapter 6).
6　Learning-centred leadership moves away from thinking about what leadership is, to focus on how leaders make a difference to teaching and learning. Recently, the NCSL introduced the term *Personalised learning-centred leadership* as well.

Activity

Go to the website www.kent.ac.uk/careers/sk/leadership.htm and try out the University of Kent's test on leadership styles. There are 50 multiple-choice questions, which can be answered quickly, to help establish the sort of leader you are.

In the following section, case studies are provided of school leaders who might be said to epitomise some of these models.

Post-transformational leadership

The first example is of a principal in Northern Ireland, where it is customary to use the terms 'principal' and 'vice principal' rather than 'head teacher' and 'deputy head teacher'. Colm Davis has tried to move his staff from a transformational view of leadership towards a more distributive style. As it takes time to change the attitudes of staff familiar with a particular way of working, the school might be said to be going through a post-transformational stage.

 Case study: Colm Davis – Special school principal in Northern Ireland

The school has 151 pupils aged 2½ to 19, who have severe learning difficulties (SLD), profound and multiple learning difficulties (PMLD), and complex learning difficulties and disabilities (CLDD). They are divided into nursery, primary, secondary and post-16. They have been waiting to move into a new building for several years and the school is now being completely rebuilt using a public–private partnership (PPP) arrangement. Colm and his staff have been able to work alongside the architects in planning the new school.

When he became the principal, Colm inherited a team of people who had been at the school for a long time. He felt that staff were not used to being involved sufficiently in decision making or encouraged to play a full part in the evolution of the school. He considered that this had limited the creativity of teachers and helped to stifle new ideas. Over the last couple of years, he has been in a position to appoint several new teachers who have been more positive about change and ready to embrace the concept of shared accountability and ownership, including a vice principal who shares his ideas. Staff have been encouraged to visit other schools and to contribute their ideas about the direction the school should take. In addition, professional development has been made a priority.

As part of a move to open up the leadership and management structure, Colm has extended the senior leadership team (SLT) to six people: principal, vice principal and four coordinators (the curriculum leaders for early years, 7–14, 14–19 and multisensory). His next step will be to broaden it further by having a coordinator for each key stage.

Colm says that it was tough running a school where the staff saw it as the sole responsibility of the principal to lead, but he has positively enjoyed changing the structure to a more distributive style of leadership and one where there is a shared sense of accountability for the success of the school and its pupils. In this, he has been supported by a vice principal who enjoys being closely involved in the decision-making process and the development of the staff.

This case study illustrates how changing attitudes is a slow process. It is not easy for staff who have been used to the style of one head, who they may have worked with for many years, to adapt to a leader with very different ideas. This adds to the challenge in taking a school forward.

Distributed leadership

A head teacher quick off the mark in seeing the opportunities in widening his leadership structure to spread responsibilities across more teachers, was Jack Hatch, whose primary school is in a town in the north-west of England. Early on, he decided that expanding the SLT would enable the school to take on a wider range of activities. As a result of a trip he made to Finland in the 1990s to see how the kindergarten system worked there, Jack returned with the idea of adapting what he had seen, to provide a more continuous educational experience right from birth up to the age of 11. This was before the advent of children's centres, but Jack says he would still take the same approach today, as there are restrictions both over the number of children's centres in any area and the locations in which they are situated.

 Case study: Jack Hatch – Head of a CE primary academy

This is a large primary school with 451 pupils aged 3–11. The head teacher is a National Leader of Education (NLE) and so the school is a National Support School (NSS). In July 2011, the school became an academy.

Before 1992, the infant and junior schools were adjacent to each other, but under different head teachers. When Jack became the first head of the combined school, his first building project was to link the schools physically, at the same time creating additional space in a school that is hemmed in on all sides by houses. Despite this restriction and the limited outdoor space, Jack has continued to extend and refurbish the school. Currently, the most recent building project is under way. This involves using sea containers to provide four additional classrooms, a studio and a playground on the roof. As Jack explains, there is no more room to build outwards, so he is going upwards instead.

Under the previous government's drive for schools to offer a wider range of services, the building was adapted to provide a foundation stage with enlarged play areas, which link to the school's nursery. In addition, the school manages a private day nursery on the site, as well as one in a neighbouring town, and is negotiating to buy another one. There are flexible arrangements for young children to move between provisions. For instance, some children attend the breakfast club and both nurseries part time, as well as after-school activities. This makes life easier for the many working parents in the area.

In recognition of the growing complexity of the school and its business interests, as well as the additional work of being an NSS, governors agreed that Jack would be called an Executive Head Teacher, and his very experienced deputy, who runs the school in his absence, would become an Executive Deputy Head. In addition, he appointed three assistant heads: one each for Foundation stage/SEN, Years 1–3 and Years 4–6.

(Continued)

(Continued)

The division between Years 1–3 and Years 4–6, rather than key stage 1 and key stage 2, is to make each assistant head responsible for three classes, and also to try to overcome the 'dip' that sometimes happens in Year 3. More recently, Jack changed one of the assistant head posts to that of junior deputy. His leadership team also includes a Commercial Manager and an Area Nursery Manager, who is in charge of all nursery provision. (There is a chart of Jack's school structure provided as a photocopiable resource in Figure 2.1 at the end of this chapter.)

Jack's reasons for wanting the school to become an academy are to have greater freedom over delivering the curriculum in a more creative manner and to ensure the school and the governors are less affected by the changing demands of national and local government.

System leadership

System leadership is a term introduced by Michael Fullan (2004), who, as has been mentioned previously, made a study of the management of change in the 1980s and 1990s. In his book, *Systems Thinkers in Action: Moving beyond the standards plateau*, he wrote that it was time for a new kind of leadership. This was followed up in 2007 by David Hopkins in his book *Every School a Great School*.

Leading a secondary federation

When Dame Yasmin Bevan arrived at a school in Luton in 1991, the school had been through many changes and, for the last seven terms, had been without a head teacher. There was a marked lack of trust between the school and the community. The first few years were spent sorting out staffing issues and appointing teachers who recognised the need to gain the confidence of the community and the importance of investing in staff training. The behaviour of the students needed to be tackled and trust built between the head and her staff, as well as between the school and the community. It took time to gain that critical mass who shared her vision of bringing out the best in every child and striving for excellence regardless of any barriers.

 Case study: Dame Yasmin Bevan – Executive principal of a secondary federation

During the time she had been head of a mixed high school, Dame Yasmin had worked closely with the head teacher of a nearby boys' high school. Both were specialist schools. The mixed school had become a sports college, which was a specialism chosen, not because it was strong in the subject, but to pull up one of the weaker areas of the curriculum, while the boys' school became a specialist science and maths school.

(Continued)

(Continued)

On the retirement three years ago of the head of the boys' school, it was agreed that the two schools would form a federation, with Dame Yasmin becoming the executive principal. As a consequence, each had an associate principal, a title chosen to illustrate a layer between that of deputy and head. In the first year, the governance layer was put in place. In the second year, there was some movement of students between the two schools and now there is joint staff training, a shared e-learning platform and a healthy collaboration to celebrate successes, ensuring that there is a feeling of collaboration rather than of rivalry between the two schools.

The schools have retained their separate governing bodies, but with the addition of a joint strategic governors' committee made up of three governors from each school. The committee structure of each governing body is the same in each school and is mirrored by the meetings of the leadership team. (A copy of the governors' and leadership meeting structure is given in Figures 2.2 and 2.3 at the end of this chapter.)

Recently, both schools have become academies and the Academy Trust also has governors from both schools. Dame Yasmin says that this model suited a particular situation and did not arise from a desire to take on a chain of schools. She explains that she went for academy status because she felt the schools were ready for further independence and wanted to be able to make their own decisions.

Both schools were involved in the development of training teachers and the boys' school is one of the first 100 schools to become a teaching school.

Dame Yasmin sees teaching schools as being very different from training schools in having a wide role in both initial teacher training (ITT) and continuing professional development (CPD). (There is more information about teaching schools in Chapter 6.) She recognises herself as someone who enjoys the challenge of change. She says: 'I love seeing opportunities; I thrive on change. You have got to make it happen yourself. Others can support you, but the choices you make are what makes the difference.'

Questions for reflection

1 What model or models of leadership is used in the school or schools with which you are familiar?
2 Do you feel that the term *system leadership* relates to your own work or the schools that you know?
3 What would you list as the positive effects of schools working more collaboratively?
4 Do you see any negative features or difficulties that may be encountered?

Styles of leadership

Moving on from models of leadership to leadership styles, Daniel Goleman et al. in their book, *Primal Leadership: Learning to lead with emotional intelligence* (2004), identify six leadership styles. While being a 'pacesetting head' can leave staff behind and a 'commanding head' may be good in a crisis, Goleman sees the four styles mosts positive in helping staff to work as a team as:

- visionary – moving people towards shared dreams
- coaching – helping individuals improve their performance
- affiliative – building relationships and dealing with problems
- democratic – helping to create a consensus by valuing everyone's input.

In a study in 2009 by Kevin Bullock for the NCSL called *The Importance of Emotional Intelligence to Effective School Leadership*, aspects that were viewed as particularly important centred on being able to:

- rise above personal differences
- bounce back from difficult situations or experiences
- deal with other people's anger effectively
- spot unrest, anxiety or anger swiftly and respond appropriately.

Leading across the services

As previously referred to, heads of today may be leading, not just wider teams within schools, but running more than one school or other types of provision. The head in the next case study is head of service at a children's resource centre, which was one of the first Early Support Pilot Programme (ESPP) Pathfinders, which helped to improve the delivery of services to disabled children under 3 years of age and their families.

Helen Norris has been a head teacher in both mainstream and special schools, before becoming the head of an extensive early years service in a London borough. She says it was this wider role that convinced her that she wanted to continue to be a head teacher, as it offered her a fresh challenge and one that she believed should happen increasingly in the future. The children's resource centre has grown significantly over the years, so that it now encompasses 26 multi-agency services that work either within or from the centre.

 Case study: Helen Norris – Head of an LA children's resource centre

The centre offers support to families with children aged 0–5 years and disability services for 0–19 years. The Head of Service, Helen Norris, is

(Continued)

(Continued)

responsible for a team of staff which includes social workers and health professionals, who work in the following teams:

- Pre-School Specialist Support and Disability Services (0–5), including a Pre-school Assessment Provision (2–5); a Portage and Pre-school Assessment Team (0–5); and the Pre-School Outreach and Inclusion Support (Early Years Provision)
- Early Support and Complex Needs Team (0–19)
- Disabled Children's Social Work and Short Break Services (incorporating the former Social Care Children's Disability Team)
- Joint Commissioning for Disabled Children.

The Pre-school Assessment Unit has four classrooms at the centre: one class is specifically for children with social communication difficulties, including some who have a diagnosis of autism, and three classes are for children who have a range of other difficulties. Outside, the space has been developed to provide outdoor play areas for all the classes and a shared area with a sensory garden and other features, such as a large engine that children can sit in, which makes it an attractive space where children can be both physically active and exercise their imaginations.

Not only is the centre a means for professionals from health, education and social care to work together, but the pre-school provision has dual workers, who are trained as both teaching assistants and medical care assistants. This makes them particularly valuable in working with some of the young children who have the most complex needs and is an example of how it may no longer be sufficient for professionals to work within tight parameters, but they should also share training across the professions.

Describing how she has adjusted her leadership style to working as head of a large, integrated service, Helen says she enjoys the stimulation of working with different colleagues, and being able to provide a joined-up service to children and their families, as well as being able to implement new ways of working, such as the training for the dual workers, who have really proved their value.

The structure of Helen's service is provided at the end of the chapter (Figure 2.4).

Helen is clear that the opportunity to develop, expand and coordinate a large multi-professional team is what has kept her interested in utilising to the full her skills as an experienced school leader.

Partnership working

Clearly, there is no one style for a successful school leader. Much will depend on people's personalities and on the demands of the setting in which they find themselves. While it is true to say that school leaders may operate very differently, what is clear is that one of the characteristics of successful leaders is their ability to adapt, to recognise the model and style of leadership that is needed and to adjust their way of working accordingly. Other characteristics are their determination, their drive and their ability to make a difference, by having a clear vision of what the school or service needs to do next and how it can be achieved. Successful leaders are people who are always striving to improve the life chances of their pupils, and, increasingly, they are concerned with the well-being and progress of other pupils as well as their own.

Further reading

Bullock, K. (2009) *The Importance of Emotional Intelligence to Effective School Leadership.* Nottingham: NCSL.

Bush, T. (2011) *Theories of Educational Leadership and Management* (4th edition). London: Sage.

Goleman, D., Boyatzis, R. and McKee, A. (2004) *Primal Leadership: Learning to lead with emotional intelligence.* Boston, MA: Harvard Business School Press.

Hopkins, D. (2007) *Every School a Great School.* Buckingham: Open University Press.

Useful website

www.kent.ac.uk/careers/sk/leadership.htm

St Bede's CE Primary Academy

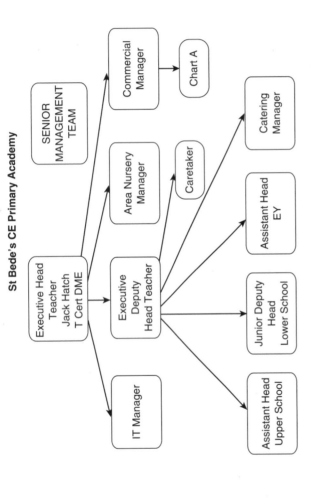

Chart A: St Bede Primary School Finance and Administration Team

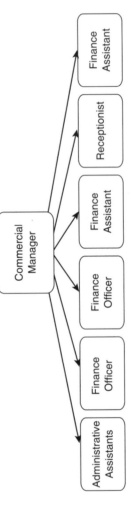

Figure 2.1 Staffing structure

Photocopiable:

How Successful Schools Work © Rona Tutt and Paul Williams, 2012

Denbigh High School and Challney High School for Boys

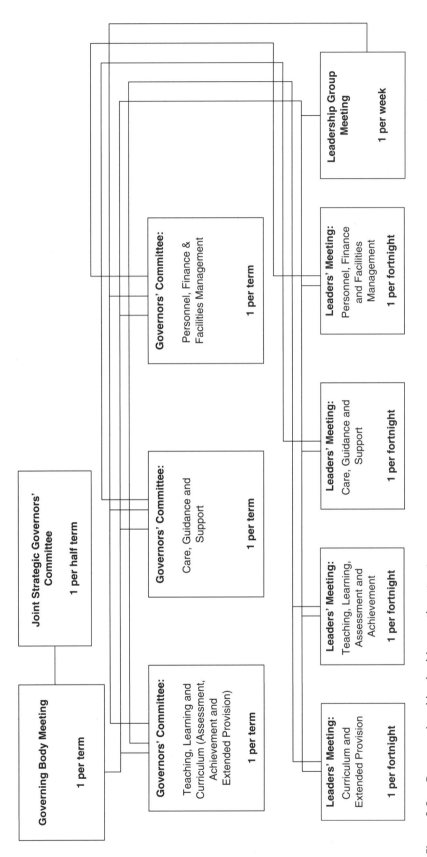

Figure 2.2 Governors' and leadership meeting structure

Photocopiable:

How Successful Schools Work © Rona Tutt and Paul Williams, 2012

Teaching, Learning and Curriculum (Assessment, Achievement and Extended Provision)

A3.1 (Provision)	The quality of teaching
A3.2 (Provision)	The use of assessment to support learning
A4.1 (L&M)	The effectiveness of leadership and management in embedding ambition and driving improvement
A4.2 (L&M)	The leadership and management of teaching and learning
A2.1 (Outcome)	Pupils' attainment
A2.2 (Outcome)	The quality of pupils' learning and their progress
A2.3 (Outcome)	The quality of learning for pupils with special educational needs and/or disabilities and their progress
A2.4 (Outcome)	Pupils' achievement and the extent to which they enjoy their learning
A3.3 (Provision)	The extent to which the curriculum meets pupils' needs, including, where relevant, through partnerships
A2.11 (Outcome)	Pupils' spiritual, moral, social and cultural development (SMSC)
A4.5 (L&M)	The effectiveness of partnerships in promoting learning and well-being
	Compliance with statutory requirements
	Self-Evaluation Form (SEF) grades

Care, Guidance and Support

A3.4 (Provision)	The effectiveness of care, guidance and support
A2.10 (Outcome)	The extent to which pupils develop workplace and other skills that contribute to their future economic well-being
A2.9 (Outcome)	Pupils' attendance
A4.4 (L&M)	The effectiveness of the school's engagement with parents and carers
A2.6 (Outcome)	Pupils' behaviour
A2.5 (Outcome)	The extent to which pupils feel safe
A4.6 (L&M)	The effectiveness with which the school promotes equal opportunity and tackles discrimination
A2.8 (Outcome)	The extent to which pupils' contribute to the school and wider community
A2.7 (Outcome)	Extent to which pupils adopt healthy lifestyles
A4.5 (L&M)	The effectiveness of partnerships in promoting learning and well-being
A4.8 (L&M)	The effectiveness with which the school promotes community cohesion
	Compliance with statutory requirements
	Self-Evaluation Form (SEF) grades

Personnel, Finance and Facilities Management

Finance	
A4.9 (L&M)	The effectiveness with which the school deploys resources to achieve value for money

Personnel	
A4.7 (L&M)	The effectiveness of safeguarding procedures

Facilities Management	
	Compliance with statutory requirement
	Self-Evaluation Form (SEF) grades

All Committees: A4.3 (L&M)

The effectiveness of the governing body in challenging and supporting the school so that weaknesses are tackled decisively and statutory responsibilities met

Figure 2.3　Governors' committee meetings 2010–2011

Photocopiable:

How Successful Schools Work © Rona Tutt and Paul Williams, 2012

Phoenix Children's Resource Centre, Bromley

Phoenix Children's Resource Centre, Bromley
Head of Service
Helen Norris
(Headteachers' conditions of service)

Finance/HR

Administration

Data and Panels

Business Support

Pre-school Specialist Support and Disability Services (0–5)
Lead
Business Support

Pre-school Assessment Provision (2–5)
Senior teacher
Teachers
Teaching assistants
Dual worker teaching/ Medical care assistants
Midday supervisors
School administration
Transport
Driver/Supervisor Escorts/Drivers

Portage and Pre-school Assessment Team (0–5)
Senior manager
Portage teachers
Portage home visitors
Resources and equipment officer
Early support
SPEACS/Early bird coordinator
Business support

Pre-school Outreach and Inclusion Support (Early Years Provision)
Senior manager
Area SEN coordinators
Inclusion development and speech and language workers
Support in Pre-Schools Service (SIPS) managers
Inclusion support workers
'Core' support workers
Business support

Joint Commissioning for Disabled Children
Joint commissioner
Complex needs and Family support worker
Placement officer
Business support

Early Support and Complex Needs (0–19)
Keyworker coordinator and senior advisory teacher
Deputy keyworker coordinator
Family liaison officer
Complex needs senior advisory teachers
Business support
Parent rep

Disabled Children's Social Work and Short Break Services
Lead
Group manager
Deputy team manager
Short break coordinator
Outreach coordinator
Information officer
Parent representative and participation officer
Senior practitioners
Social workers
Social work assistants
Business support

Figure 2.4   Specialist Support and Disability Services organisational structure

Photocopiable:
How Successful Schools Work © Rona Tutt and Paul Williams, 2012

3

Leading inclusive environments

> **Chapter overview**
>
> This chapter examines the different meanings of inclusion and how schools are finding ways of becoming more inclusive, whether this is about including children with special educational needs and disabilities (SEND), or making sure that children of all backgrounds, languages and cultures feel equally valued.
>
> There are case studies of schools that serve to illustrate the continuum of SEND provision, including one in Scotland, as well as a case study of an Integrated College in Northern Ireland, where being integrated refers to not being segregated along sectarian lines.

Definitions

Inclusion is a word with many meanings. In terms of children and young people with special educational needs and disabilities (SEND), there is a long history of the battle between those who believe that all children should be in mainstream schools and those who have recognised the need to have a continuum of provision. Happily, there is now a consensus on having the full range of provision, including special schools and other forms of specialist provision.

Inclusion also has wider connotations, as it can be applied to any groups who are in danger of feeling marginalised. The term additional support needs (ASN) is used in Scotland to cover both pupils with SEND and this wider group. The chapter illustrates some of the ways in which the term is used, including the concept of integration in the context of schools in Northern Ireland.

Including pupils with SEND

Throughout the 1980s and 1990s, there was a drive to have more pupils with SEN educated in mainstream schools. However, the turn of the century saw a more pragmatic view being taken. The government's SEN strategy,

Removing Barriers to Achievement (DfES, 2004b), shifted the argument from talking about the closure of special schools, to giving them a dual role: educating those with the most complex needs, and working with local schools to meet the needs of the wider population of pupils with SEND.

In 2007, when he was minister for SEN, Andrew Adonis said that the government wished to see local authorities (LAs) maintain *a flexible range of provision*. Subsequently, a guidance document, *Planning and Developing Special Educational Provision* (DCSF, 2007c), was published, stating that before dismantling any type of specialist provision, LAs should be able to demonstrate that the changes would lead to an improvement in provision.

A focus on SEND

The years 2007 to 2011 showed a growing interest in the whole field of SEND, a growth which continued through a change of government. This is evidenced by the number of reports on different conditions that were issued at this time, including: Steer's work on behaviour (DCSF, 2009d; DfES, 2005); Bercow's (2008) report on speech language and communication needs (SLCN); the Child and Adolescent Mental Health Service's (CAMHS) report on mental health issues (DCSF/DoH, 2008); Rose's (2006) review of dyslexia and literacy difficulties; and Salt's (DCSF, 2010) review into the supply of teachers for pupils with severe learning difficulties (SLD) and profound and multiple learning difficulties (PMLD).

 Activity

To support schools in understanding how to meet pupils' needs, the government asked the National Strategies (since disbanded) to produce an Inclusion Development Programme (IDP). This has online training materials for speech, language and communication needs (SLCN), dyslexia, autism and behavioural, emotional and social difficulties (BESD).

Go to the site below and explore any of the materials which interest you and with which you are unfamiliar. They are designed as online training for all staff: www.nasentraining.org.uk/resources

Overlapping and co-existing disorders

Recently, there has been a move to look at children more holistically and to recognise the fact that children can have overlapping and co-existing disorders. This was the theme of a book by Dittrich and Tutt in 2008, in which they concentrated on the four neurological disorders of autism, ADHD (attention deficit hyperactivity disorder), specific language impairment

(SLI) and the specific learning difficulties (SpLD) of dyslexia, dyspraxia, dyscalculia and dysgraphia. In 2009 to 2011, there was a government-funded research project on educating pupils with complex learning difficulties and disabilities (CLDD), which also focused on children with co-existing conditions. (Further details are given in the next chapter.)

Additional support needs (ASN)

The first case study in this chapter is about a primary school in Scotland, where ASN is a much wider term than SEND.

 Key points: Additional support needs (ASN)

Scotland recognises:

- motor or sensory impairments
- emotional and social difficulties
- learning difficulties.

But, in addition, the following categories come under ASN:

- being bullied
- being particularly able or talented
- having experienced a bereavement
- being looked after by the local authority
- living with parents who are abusing substances, or who have mental health problems
- having English as a second language
- not attending school regularly
- being on the child protection register
- being young carers.

In England, great care is taken to separate out children who do not have English as their first language and those who have SEND (unless, of course, it is clear that a child has a learning difficulty that is not due to their unfamiliarity with the English language). However, by using the broader term of ASN and specifying the separate categories within it, these problems might be said to be overcome.

 Questions for reflection

1 What do you think might be the advantages of using the broader term of ASN?
2 Do you see any disadvantages? If so, what are they?

(Continued)

(Continued)

3 If the term ASN were to be preferred to SEND, are there any other groups of pupils you feel should be included?

4 Is there another term to SEND or ASN that you would prefer? If so, what would it be and who would it cover?

A primary school in East Lothian

In 2008, when a new primary school was being built, the East Lothian authority took the opportunity to include a range of facilities under one roof, including discrete provision within the school for pupils who have severe and complex additional needs. This enabled the head teacher, Fiona Waddell, and her three depute heads, particularly Anne Cockburn, to plan for a school that, in a sense, goes beyond co-location. (Primary pupils in Scotland start at the same age as in England, but they stay until they are 12. The classes are named P1 to P7.)

 Case study: Fiona Waddell – Head teacher of a primary school in E. Lothian; Anne Cockburn – Depute head with responsibility for the specialist provision

The school has provision for 470 pupils, including 120 in the nursery (60 in the morning and 60 in the afternoon) and 16 in the specialist provision. Under the same roof is a wraparound care facility, an early years centre, a youth club and a wing for community activities, with space for health visitors, Home Start, Community Learning and Development, and other professionals from health and social care. Also accommodated are two children's charities: Children 1st (formerly known as the Royal Scottish Society for Prevention of Cruelty to Children [RSSPCC]) and the Place2Be (a charity working with schools to improve children's well-being). All the elements are joined together in a rectangular shape around a large central outdoor space, which has been divided into different playground areas, made attractive for play and outdoor learning, with grass, flowers and herbs, as well as playground equipment. The school also runs a breakfast club, an after-school club and wrap-around provision.

The senior management team (SMT) consists of the head and three depute heads: one for early years, one for the upper school and Anne Cockburn, who is in charge of the specialist provision. Staff meetings take place between all the staff, as well as separate ones for the main school and the severe and complex additional needs provision.

Children in this provision, as well as having their own classrooms in one of the wings, are attached to peer group classes, where they spend varying amounts of time depending on their needs. All the children in P5 and P6 learn Signalong, a simplified signing system (similar to Makaton), to help

(Continued)

(Continued)

them communicate with children who are non-verbal, or whose understanding is enhanced by signing. In addition, reverse integration takes place, when children in P7 act as volunteer buddies and get to know the pupils with complex needs, by working with them in their own setting. Some learn to be trainers and teach others to sign. They run workshops for parents and community groups, including the police and supermarket staff. As well as honing their signing, this helps them to develop the skills involved in presenting to different groups. Arrangements are also made for the pupils with complex needs to spend time with their local primary schools, so that they do not lose contact with their home communities.

Anne has noticed that more pupils are entering the school with complex health needs, due to premature births, rare syndromes and an increase in numbers with autism. The provision has a high staffing level based on the needs of the individual pupils. Anne and her staff have found the Engagement Profile and Engagement Scale that have been developed recently for pupils with severe, profound and complex learning difficulties and disabilities, a very useful addition to the approaches they already use. (The Engagement Scale and Profile are mentioned more fully in the next chapter.)

When one of the pupils left to move on to secondary school, she took the trouble to write and say 'thank you', adding a comment on what it meant to her to be at a primary school which included provision for children with complex needs. She wrote: 'It's taught me that everyone is the same.'

Current perspectives on SEND

At the time of a change of government in England, two significant publications that looked at the SEND system rather than focusing on needs, were the *Lamb Inquiry: Special educational needs and parental confidence* (DCSF, 2009c) and Ofsted's *The Special Educational Needs and Disability Review: A statement is not enough*, which was published in September 2010. The inspectors made it clear that the setting the child was in was less important than the quality of teaching they received.

The SEND Green Paper

These were followed by the government's Green Paper, *Support and Aspiration: A new approach to special educational needs and disability* (DfE, 2011a). This document has been described as the biggest shake-up of the SEND system since the Warnock Report (DES, 1978). It appeared in March 2011 and drew on the findings of many of the documents already mentioned, as well as the Conservative's Commission on Special Needs in Education, which began in 2005.

The main proposals in the Green Paper include:

- replacing statements with an Education, Health and Care Plan (EHCP) that would cover 0–25 years of age
- giving parents personal budgets, better information on what is available locally, and the right to express a preference for any type of state-funded school
- replacing School Action and School Action Plus with a single category
- rolling out the Achievement for All (AfA) project, as a way of raising the achievement of the 20 per cent lowest-attaining pupils. (More details of AfA and a corresponding case study are given in Chapter 6.)

Some elements of the Green Paper are being piloted by LAs between September 2011 and July 2013. However, legislative changes are due to be made from May 2012 onwards.

Creating a special school from scratch

Some specialist provision is provided by non-maintained and independent special schools. Sometimes, these schools are for the most complex end of the SEND continuum, not necessarily meaning for those with the greatest cognitive difficulties, but for those at the severe end of a particular type of need, in the case of the next school highlighted, BESD.

From the start, the founder, Sue Tinson, wanted to ensure that the school she was establishing was soundly based and would add to the knowledge about how to create a successful environment for girls who had failed elsewhere, and whose chaotic and negative experiences to date had created significant barriers to learning. With this in mind, Sue entered into a Knowledge Transfer Partnership (KTP) with Southampton University so that an outside observer would be able to view at first hand the effect the education being offered was having on the students (see Clarke et al., 2010; Nind et al., 2011).

Having been a Looked After Child (LAC) and having had a rather chequered career as a pupil herself, Sue was determined to do something about the lack of provision for girls exhibiting extremely challenging behaviour. After training as a teacher and gaining experience, including four years teaching in a pupil referral unit (PRU), she decided it was time to start her own school.

 Case study: Sue Tinson – Founder and principal of an independent school for girls with BESD

The school opened in 2006 in a converted detached house in a city suburb. It caters mainly for secondary-age pupils up to the age of 16, but can take pupils from 9 years of age. Since January 2010, the school has been able to

(Continued)

(Continued)

offer residential placements in two other houses, which are registered as children's homes, so that they can be open all year. Around half the pupils are in care and have had many disruptions in their lives. Others have been drawn into drugs, drink and early sexual encounters. All have exhibited extremely challenging behaviour and been excluded from one or more schools, but respond positively to a family environment where everyone is respected regardless of what has happened before they arrive. The school's motto is: 'The past is something that's gone forever; the future is something we will work on together.'

Because of the small size of the school, it is possible to offer a personalised curriculum. Sue says she has been able to mould the curriculum around the girls rather than the other way round, and because their needs are so complex and individual, this is the only way to get them back on track. Although such provision is bound to be expensive, Sue argues that the money spent now is cost-effective in the longer term. She says: 'The main ingredient is respect. The girls' needs are all different, but the one thing that works for all of them is respect.'

Sue goes on to explain that respect is at the heart of the way everyone is treated. This means there is no feeling of 'them and us', but an emphasis on learning to form relationships based on trust. Students feel they are listened to and their voices heard. Everything in the environment, from furniture to computers, is top quality, so that everyone feels valued. Mornings are spent on academic subjects, with an emphasis on literacy and maths, while the afternoons are filled with the creative arts and physical activity. Therapy forms part of the curriculum, with all students having My Time, where they can receive counselling, psychoanalytic therapy, or support from a health and well-being instructor.

Around 80 per cent of the pupils start part-time college courses while they are still at the school and move on to college full-time when they leave, something they might not have envisaged themselves doing when they first arrived. Sue explains that it is a question of looking at the whole picture, not just education, but the rest of their lives, and seeing it in terms of the past, present and future. She and her staff do not want simply to contain them for a short while, but to look at the future and how they can be helped to achieve their potential.

Sue says the pupils have to learn that they cannot behave in a way that does not recognise boundaries, so it is a question of helping them to take responsibility for their behaviour, and then working with them – and their families and other agencies involved – to remove the barriers, one by one, that stand in the way of their ability to learn. (Photocopiable pages showing how the school involves the students in target setting, is given at the end of the chapter in Figure 3.1.)

Including the school in the wider community

There are many schools, both primary and secondary, that have changed how they work to meet new demands in terms of a changing population in the locality. This goes much wider than SEND and includes the needs of pupils from diverse cultures and backgrounds, encouraging them all to see the school and the education it offers as central to their lives. This has meant reaching out to communities in a way that, in the past, might not have been seen as part of a school's role, but is now recognised by many as the key to raising standards.

One such school is run by Kenny Frederick, where the head and her staff have gone out of their way to create harmony and understanding in an area that was riven by suspicion and mistrust, both within the school and in the community it serves. Kenny decided to take the radical step of sending 60 students at a time to Belfast, which helped them to gain a fresh perspective and a desire to become more integrated, with the pupils themselves deciding to form a Unity Team and taking a leading role in bringing the school factions together and making the school part of the local community.

 ### Case study: Kenny Frederick – Head of an inner city comprehensive school

This voluntary controlled school is a multi-cultural, multi-racial community of over 1200 pupils aged 11–19, which has nearly doubled in size since Kenny took over 15 years ago. It is in a community with high levels of social and economic disadvantage, with well above average numbers of students on free school meals (FSM), half of minority ethnic origin and over a third with SEND. The head and her staff have worked tirelessly to forge good relationships with the local community, so that everyone feels included in the life of the school. This is one of the reasons why the school became a humanities college in 2006, specialising in English, Citizenship and Drama.

The school's extensive work in the community includes taking on responsibility for the provision of youth services, which it has been commissioned to lead by the local authority. This has become an integral part of the school's work. The school runs an extended day and is open until 10pm each evening, so staff work flexible hours. It makes use of counsellors, a family therapist, final-year social work students, as well as complex needs support from teaching assistants for pupils with SEND. Older pupils act as mentors to younger ones. There is a community policeman and a team of supervisors, known by the children as Redcoats (because of their uniform), who are on hand patrolling the corridors, not just to sort out problems, but to be aware of any child who is unhappy or distressed. Students themselves have contributed to improving behaviour, for instance through their work on an anti-bullying committee, and all these measures have helped to provide a safe environment for everyone.

Students also play a key role in the school's development. There is a teaching and learning student committee and pupils partner with teachers to observe their lessons and give regular feedback, having been trained in

(Continued)

(Continued)

lesson observation using Ofsted's criteria. The idea of learning walks, which are often used by school leaders as another form of lesson observation, has been extended to include people from the local community, so that they can visit classes and see the school at work.

Partly because of the nature of its intake, Kenny made the decision to offer the International Baccalaureate (IB) as an alternative to A-level, an option that has proved to be popular with students. (Further details of the school's approach to the IB are given in the next chapter.) Kenny and her leadership team have worked hard on providing a curriculum to re-engage disaffected learners by offering them a greater degree of choice. Kenny stresses that pupils need to know that equal opportunities is not about treating everybody the same, but about appreciating and celebrating their individual strengths and gifts. The school's motto is: 'We are all different and all equal'.

After many difficult years of trying to bring together a divided community, Kenny says: 'I get a buzz out of doing something different, but you need resilience to survive.' She works closely with the primary schools around her and says: 'I want this school to succeed, but not at the expense of others, because I want all schools to succeed.'

Other meanings of integration and inclusion

Some of the case studies featured in this book are from Northern Ireland, where the word 'integration' takes on a different meaning. As mentioned previously, while special schools admit pupils from all religious backgrounds, other schools adopt either a Protestant or Catholic ethos and, as such, pupils generally enrol in the school adhering to their own religious beliefs. However, a minority are integrated schools and the next case study features a principal of an integrated school.

An integrated college in Northern Ireland

Andrew Sleeth was appointed Leader of Mathematics in an integrated college when it opened in 1995. In 2004, the principal was seconded to the Regional Training Unit (RTU) (which has a similar role to the NCSL in England), and Andrew became acting principal before becoming the principal two years later. This is one of 20 integrated colleges and Andrew has sought to ensure that the college is part of the local community of schools, encouraging local people to use the college and its library, as well as other areas that have been made available for renting out. Within the college itself, he has instigated several ways in which every student feels valued and able to contribute to the school and to the wider community.

Case study: Andrew Sleeth – Principal of an integrated college in Northern Ireland

The college's motto is 'Alumni in Sociis', meaning 'Learning Together', continuing the theme of the Northern Ireland Council for Integrated Education's motto: 'Educating Children Together'. This is the coordinating body for integrated education, to which the school belongs. The principal says it summarises a belief that 'all children should be taught together: boys and girls, Protestant and Catholic, other faiths or none, children with or without disabilities'.

The college is part of the local Area Learning Community, which encourages schools to work together to deliver GCSE and post-16 courses. This enables students to move between schools to find the combination of courses they need. Andrew is hoping to coordinate a similar approach for GCSE students. As well as its links at post-primary level, the college has partnerships with three integrated primary schools, a special school and two schools in Riyhad, Saudi Arabia.

The active involvement of students of all ages contributes to their sense of belonging and being able to contribute to the school and wider community. Student voice is a strong feature. Not only does every class have student councillors to represent them on the student council, but the chair and vice chair play a full part on the college's governing body. Andrew says they have been very persuasive when putting a case to governors, for instance in convincing them to spend money on upgrading the school canteen and to change the colour of the college jumper and tie. Andrew checks through the agenda for the student council meetings and meets them afterwards to go through the minutes.

The school has found that the 'restorative justice' approach has helped to avoid conflict. A team of sixth-formers have been trained in the method and, in recognition of their work, received the Diana Anti-bullying Award. One visible effect of this emphasis on improving relationships and behaviour has been that Saturday detentions were reduced and then abandoned altogether, as they were no longer needed. (Further information about restorative justice and the college's approach to it is given in Chapter 5.)

Andrew believes in reducing the terminal exam overload on students and has measures in place to share assessment and pastoral information with parents regularly. He is pleased that inspectors welcome this approach, which they have described as showing the college is *information rich rather than data rich*.

Andrew and his staff have worked hard at giving students the opportunity to enrich their education by having over 50 extra-curricular activities to draw on. As well as being able to spend extra time on study, they can try their hand at activities such as being involved in a French boules club, an ice cream club, a Portuguese language club, a rugby club, a ladies Gaelic football club and a golf club.

The college's vision is summarised under the four headings of: Ethos, Education, Enrichment, Everyone.

Qualities of school leaders in different settings

Leaders in specialist provision often remark that they have to know what is happening in mainstream schools as well as knowing how to adapt everything to the particular needs of their pupils. Those that are all-age special schools also have the added pressure of knowing about the curriculum for all key stages. On the other hand, they are usually dealing with significantly smaller numbers of pupils, although not necessarily of staff.

What is becoming clear, however, in this and in previous chapters, is a similarity of approach in being innovative in carving out new approaches to meeting pupils' needs, in delivering the curriculum and in including the voice of the pupils themselves, their families and the wider community, in the life of the school. The question of how far innovative leaders have characteristics in common that enable them to lead successful schools will be returned to in the final chapter. The next chapter picks up the idea of exploring new pedagogies as part of looking at the power invested in school leaders.

Further reading

Department for Children, Schools and Families (DCSF) (2009c) *Lamb Inquiry: Special educational needs and parental confidence.* Nottingham: DCSF Publications.

Department for Education (DfE) (2011a) *Support and Aspiration: A new approach to special educational needs and disability.* Nottingham: DfE Publications.

Dittrich, W. and Tutt, R. (2008) *Educating Children with Complex Conditions: Understanding overlapping and co-existing disorders.* London: Sage.

Ofsted (2010b) *The Special Educational Needs and Disability Review: A statement is not enough.* Manchester: Ofsted Publications.

Useful website

www.nasentraining.org.uk/resources

The Serendipity Centre

<u>R</u>espect <u>E</u>ffort <u>A</u>chievement <u>P</u>articipate

| Day | M | T | W | T | F | Date | 1 | 2 | 3 | 4 | 5 | 6 | 7 | 8 | 9 | 10 | 11 | 12 | 13 | 14 | 15 | 16 | 17 | 18 | 19 | 20 | 21 | 22 | 23 | 24 | 25 | 26 | 27 | 28 | 29 | 30 | 31 | Month | 1 | 2 | 3 | 4 | 5 | 6 | 7 | 8 | 9 | 10 | 11 | 12 |

IEP

1	2	3
-------------------	-------------------	-------------------
-------------------	-------------------	-------------------
-------------------	-------------------	-------------------

My Body

Food & Drink

Fruit & Veg

Cold Drinks

Hot Drinks

Exercise

Description

Duration

My Health

Cigarettes		
My Signs		
Medicines		
Teeth	am	pm
My Time		hours

My Self

Observations am
StartRight

Break

Observations pm
Lunch

Registration

Comments

My Learning

	R	E	A	P	1	2	3	B	Comments	Staff	Total
Uniform	U	U	U	U							
StartRight	R	E	S	T							
Breakfast	R	E	S	T							
1	R	E	A	P							
2	R	E	A	P							
Break	R	E	S	T							
3	R	E	A	P							
4	R	E	A	P							
Lunch	R	E	S	T							
5	R	E	A	P							
6	R	E	A	P							
Tutor	R	E	S	T							
Totals											

Achievements

My World

Participation in
School Community

Participation in
Local Community

Comments

My Future

Learning for
Independence

Learning for Leisure

Learning About Money
£

Learning About Work

Homework Bonus

Respect:

Phone

Yes / No

Top Up

Voucher

(Continued)

(Continued)

<u>R</u>espect <u>E</u>ffort <u>A</u>chievement <u>P</u>articipate

| Day | M | T | W | T | F | Date | 1 | 2 | 3 | 4 | 5 | 6 | 7 | 8 | 9 | 10 | 11 | 12 | 13 | 14 | 15 | 16 | 17 | 18 | 19 | 20 | 21 | 22 | 23 | 24 | 25 | 26 | 27 | 28 | 29 | 30 | 31 | Month | 1 | 2 | 3 | 4 | 5 | 6 | 7 | 8 | 9 | 10 | 11 | 12 |

Subject	HOMEWORK	
	---	Due Completed ☐
	---	Due Completed ☐
	---	Due Completed ☐
	---	Due Completed ☐

Accidents Please tell us about any incidents	Incidents Please tell us about any incidents
--------------------------------------- --------------------------------------- --------------------------------------- ---------------------------------------	--------------------------------------- --------------------------------------- --------------------------------------- ---------------------------------------

Please tell us if there is anything else we should know, or you would like to know

----

Figure 3.1   Target-setting chart

Photocopiable:

How Successful Schools Work © Rona Tutt and Paul Williams, 2012

The power of leadership

> **Chapter overview**
>
> This chapter discusses the power that is attached to positions of leadership and the right and wrong way it can be used within educational settings.
>
> The first case study is of a school where the head teacher had to work within the constraints generated by political decisions made at the local level.
>
> The other three case studies are of head teachers' power to influence the curriculum and pedagogy, leading to approaches as diverse as the International Primary Curriculum (IPC), 'Opening Minds' and the use of neuroscience to benefit children with complex learning difficulties.

The pendulum swing of power

After the 1988 Education Act, the autonomy enjoyed previously was trimmed, as school leaders had to make sure the national curriculum was followed, that their schools' reputation did not suffer from poor test and examination results and that they were in a constant state of readiness for the next inspection. Local authorities (LAs) also took a greater interest in what their schools were up to, as *their* reputation was on the line as well.

At the moment, much of the curriculum is in a state of flux, with the early years foundation stage (EYFS) to post-16 being at various stages of review. However, the government has said that it wants schools to have more freedom, as shown by the rise in academies and allowing free schools to flourish. This creates a very different picture as regards the relationship between LAs and schools, and places more power in the hands of school leaders, who, with their governors, can decide the type of school they want to run, the relationship they wish to have with their LA, and what the curriculum and pedagogical approach should be.

Not all countries give school leaders as much freedom. In his book, *Schools Must Speak for Themselves* (1999), John MacBeath points out that primary schools in Switzerland have no head teacher; Danish schools believe in a 'flatarchy' and shared leadership; and Dutch schools are grouped in clusters, where leadership is not seen as a significant factor.

The rewards and dangers of power

School leaders have power over many people's lives – the staff who work with them, their pupils and their families, and the many other contacts they make every day as part of their role. The rewards of being in such a position can be considerable, but used wrongly, that power can make others miserable and lead to an unpleasant and unproductive atmosphere.

Essentially, what school leaders need in order to use power well is to have a high level of self-awareness, so that they are very conscious of how their actions impact on those around them. In other words, they need to be emotionally intelligent. This term was used in Chapter 2 with reference to different styles of leadership. Here, it is being used in terms of what makes an emotionally intelligent leader.

Emotional intelligence

The term *emotional intelligence* came into use after Goleman's book, *Emotional Intelligence: Why it can matter more than IQ*, was published in 1996. Emotional intelligence, as described by Goleman, has five main domains:

- self-awareness – understanding your own strengths and weaknesses
- self-regulation – believing in being held personally accountable and staying in control
- motivation – having high standards and being consistent about what you are trying to achieve
- empathy – being able to inspire loyalty in others and wanting to develop all members of the team
- social skills – making others feel enthusiastic about change and managing conflicts well.

School leaders of today need a high level of emotional intelligence, in order to carry people with them as they tread in unchartered waters, while the world around them evolves at an ever-increasing pace.

Political power

Of course, school leaders must operate within the parameters set by national and local government. The first case study in this chapter is about the experience of Raymond McFeeters, who was appointed to bring three special schools together under one roof, to form the largest special school in Northern Ireland. After he was appointed, the building to accommodate the three schools was put on hold, due to changes on the political front and as a response to the downturn in the economy. Although he still hopes that, one day, the money and the political will might be there, in the meantime, he has had to blend the three schools into a single entity, while each remains on its original site. Raymond has kept the original names of the three schools, but has called them campuses instead of schools, with all three operating under a single name for the new school. There are 270 pupils across the new school, which has a single governing body. (In Northern Ireland, children transfer at Year 7 rather than Year 6.)

 Case study: Raymond McFeeters – Principal of a special school in Northern Ireland

In September 2007, Raymond was appointed to oversee the amalgamation of the three schools and to create a new leadership and management structure. Although the pupils have had to remain on their previous sites, he has tried to make the pupils feel as if they belong to the same school, by introducing a common badge and uniform, and by having pupils and staff moving freely between the campuses. Two of the previous schools are on the same site, while the third is a short journey away. The campuses provide for the following types of difficulty:

- pupils who have moderate learning difficulties, covering the whole of the age range (key stages 1–4), with a life skills unit for the 16+ age group
- pupils with physical difficulties aged pre-school to Year 7, after which they transfer to mainstream provision or to a different special school
- pupils with severe learning difficulties (SLD), covering key stages 1–4.

In order to effect a smooth transition from three separate schools under their own principals, in the first year, Raymond appointed a head of each school with himself as the overarching principal. He has now moved to the next stage of having a senior team that goes across the three schools. He has two vice principals, one for director of curriculum and a director of personal care, plus a deputy vice principal who is head of outreach and planning. A member of staff from Health joins the SLT for some meetings. In addition, there are working groups led by the SLT, which go across the campuses. Teachers working in the same key stage have Planning Partners, so that they can share ideas and planning is consistent. In these ways, Raymond has tried to give both the staff and the pupils a sense of belonging to one school, while they have to remain physically separate, at least for now.

Raymond chairs the local Learning Together partnership, which includes two grammar schools. The group focuses on community relations, helping to bring different groups of children together, at the same time as breaking down any barriers between special and mainstream schools. Joint INSET days take place and Raymond's school has run workshops for over 500 mainstream teachers.

Power to deliver the curriculum

At the present time, the government in England is using *its* power to take a fresh look at the curriculum for all ages. Although it is not yet clear what the outcome will be of all the reviews, the government's declared intention is to reduce the extent of the national curriculum. In addition, greater recognition is being given to the International Baccalaureate (IB) as an alternative to A-levels, as well as to the International General Certificate of Education (iGCSE) and the International Primary Curriculum (IPC).

As teaching and learning are the heart of what schools do, innovative school leaders are seizing the opportunity to deliver the curriculum in a more creative way. The following case studies are of a primary, a secondary and a special school head teacher, who are using the power they have to determine the curriculum that is right for their school.

A primary example

Anne McCormick decided in 2006 to adopt the IPC as an added dimension to the national curriculum.

 Key points: International Primary Curriculum (IPC)

The IPC was launched in 2000 to provide an international curriculum for a group of 14 schools around the world. Currently, the IPC is followed by 1000 schools in 65 different countries.

It was introduced into the UK in 2003 and 700 primary schools now follow it.

The IPC is a thematic curriculum, and the topics are divided into Early Years, Milestone 1 (5–7 years), Milestone 2 (7–9 years) and Milestone 3 (9–12 years).

The principle behind it is to provide a combination of academic, personal and international learning, presented in a way that appeals to pupils.

Anne's school is in a unitary authority that has the three-tier system of lower, middle and upper schools. In January 2004, the school admitted children from a closing neighbouring school and in September that year, the school was reorganised, with Years 1–4 in the main school building and the Foundation Stage on a nearby early years site.

 Case study: Anne McCormick – Head of a lower school academy

Anne's school is in a county town in the home counties. It has a very diverse population and the majority of children enter the nursery with English as their second language. There are 554 pupils on roll. Bangladeshi and Pakistani families are the largest groups, with 10 per cent White British and the rest from countries as varied as India, Africa, the Caribbean, Poland, Portugal and Afghanistan. Anne is a National Leader of Education (NLE) and the school's role as a National Support School (NSS) has involved them in

(Continued)

(Continued)

working alongside schools beyond the LA, including a 'hard federation' of two schools in another unitary authority. Anne has changed the structure of her leadership team, so that it includes three Heads of School, who work across all three schools to deliver improvement. With a middle and an upper school, Anne's school forms the town's first Full Service Extended School.

Anne has organised her school so that all the children and staff are members of one of four World Families – Africa, America, Asia and Australia. Two children from Year 4 are chosen to be the 'Head of the World Family'. Each week, the heads of the world families meet as a children's panel to consider any child whose behaviour is impacting negatively on the learning of others. A restorative justice approach is applied. (There is a fuller explanation of this approach in Chapter 5.) In addition, each of the Years 1–4 elects a representative to sit on the Student Leadership Team, together with the heads of the world families. They consider school life from the pupils' perspective and advise the Senior Leadership Team of their findings. Anne describes them as a valued asset to the school.

In September 2005, the school introduced the International Primary Curriculum (IPC) for Years 1–4 and the school has established a link with a primary school in China. Anne sees the IPC as providing a thematic approach to the foundation subjects of the national curriculum, which both challenges and motivates the pupils, inspiring them to excel and to achieve. English and Maths are now taught within the themes, where relevant and appropriate. In addition, the school follows a values-based approach to education, working on a different theme each month. (A list of these themes is given in the next chapter.)

Anne's emphasis on pupil involvement and the international dimension to the school's work, are part of her belief that there must be trust and mutual respect if people are to live and work alongside each other.

The secondary curriculum

At the end of key stage 4, the majority of students take their GCSEs, although a growing number are considering the iGCSE (or IGSE). For 16–19-year-olds, more schools are offering the IB. In the previous chapter, one of the case studies was of Kenny Frederick, whose school uses the IB as the core of their sixth-form curriculum. She explained that the IB fully supports the school's central aim of inclusion. At her school, there is a two-year plan around the IB's six themes. (An overview of the school's approach is given in Figures 4.1, 4.2 and 4.3 at the end of this chapter.)

Key points: International Baccalaureate (IB)

The IB was founded in Geneva in 1968 and works with over 3000 schools in over 140 countries. The programmes are designed to encourage students

(Continued)

(Continued)

from across the world to be lifelong learners, who will create a more peace-ful world through greater understanding and respect.

Although the IB offers three programmes, covering primary (3–12) and middle (11–16), it is best known for the Diploma that is an alternative to A-levels. Students choose from six areas of study, and, in addition, they write an extended essay requiring research, follow a course on the theory of knowledge and engage in active learning beyond the classroom.

Wales has its own version, known as the Welsh Baccalaureate, which follows a similar model.

The school in the next case study also gives its students the option of study-ing for the IB, alongside a different approach to teaching and learning.

A secondary case study

The RSA Academy is a school that offers a wide range of qualifications to its students at both key stage 4 and key stage 5, as well as an innovative peda-gogical approach known as 'Opening Minds'.

Key points: Opening Minds

Opening Minds is an approach based on the five competencies of:

1 Citizenship
2 Learning
3 Managing information
4 Relating to people
5 Managing situations

It is more to do with *how* to teach rather than being a curriculum in its own right.

It was developed by the RSA and is now put into practice by the RSA Academy as well as by 200 schools elsewhere in England.

Note: RSA stands for the *Royal Society for the Encouragement of Arts, Manufactures and Commerce*, a charitable organisation with a long history of involvement in education.

One of the people involved in developing Opening Minds is Lesley James, who used to work at the RSA. When the Academy was established, she moved to become its Director of Business Development, which includes leading on Opening Minds and seeing the theory put into practice. The Academy is organised into three schools or faculties. The Senior Leadership Team includes the principal, executive vice principal and three directors of schools: the Director for Arts, Humanities, Sports and Leisure; the Director for Language and Communication; and the Director for Maths, Science and Technology.

Case study: Lesley James – Director of Business Development, RSA Academy

The academy has 1100 pupils aged 11–19. It opened under its principal, Michael Gernon, in 2008 in the premises of the school it replaced and moved to its new building on the same site in August 2010. It runs a five-term year, with each term being about eight weeks. There is a break in the morning for students and staff to have breakfast together, followed by a three-hour lesson in the morning and another one in the afternoon. The three-hour lessons are designed to provide time to explore a subject or theme in depth. The academy stays open until 6.30pm for students and until 10pm for the community to enjoy its facilities. This has helped to increase parental interest in the school and in their children's education. This is very important in a locality where pupils are very largely from White working-class families and the area is recognised as one of considerable deprivation. The hospitality department caters for evening events, giving practical experience in catering to some of the students, while the media team records school events, again providing scope for Media Studies' students to hone their practical skills. The school makes a point of phoning parents to pass on good news, rather than just to report incidents of poor behaviour.

Opening Minds

Key stage 3 covers Years 7 and 8 (rather than 7 to 9) and the competencies are taught across all subjects. The first objective for each lesson is about the competency being covered. As the approach is qualitative, guidelines are drawn up showing how to assess students' progress, and part of this will be based on students' self-assessment of the progress they have made. At key stages 4 and 5, staff look at how to balance work on the competencies with the content to be covered in each exam subject. (As key stage 4 starts in Year 9, most GCSEs are taken in Year 10.) The hope is that the competencies will help students to cope with exams and to get better results. This is already happening with improved results at key stage 3, where it is becoming clear that students understand the competencies and feel they own their learning. There are three pathways at key stage 4: GCSEs; a mixture of GCSEs and other courses; and alternatives to GCSEs including ASDAN (Award Scheme Development and Accreditation Network), to ensure all students can follow appropriate courses. In addition, they all study for at least one BTEC.

Currently, the academy is working with ASDAN to develop an Opening Minds certificate for students. It is also involved in piloting the IB Career-Related Certificate (IBCC). An accreditation programme has been developed, so that other schools can be recognised for the quality of their Opening Minds curriculum. Lesley says that the approach all along has been about interesting and engaging students and their families in education as well as making them better learners. She says the questions they have sought to answer are: 'What can we do to make learning real and what can we do to bring those outside into the academy?'

Pedagogy and complex needs

For some pupils at the most complex end of the SEND continuum, a lack of knowledge about how they learn, has made it hard to educate them using traditional methods.

From 2009 to 2011, a complex learning difficulties and disabilities (CLDD) research project, led by Barry Carpenter, encouraged teachers in the project schools to take an inquiry-based approach (sometimes referred to as a problem-based approach). From here, an Engagement Profile and an Engagement Scale were developed (see Figures 4.4 and 4.5 at the end of this chapter). Further details about using these resources are available on The SSAT/Schools Network website (http://complexld.ssatrust.org.uk). David Braybrook, who quality assured the project, suggested that taking this approach had meant that the staff involved had been able to move from 'intrusion to inclusion'.

Case study of a CLDD project school in Wales

As well as the school in Scotland mentioned in the previous chapter, another of the schools involved as a project school is in Pembrokeshire. The head teacher, Sue Painter, has worked for both Ofsted and Estyn (the inspection system in Wales). In common with many innovative heads, she has overseen the development of the only special school in the authority from 40 pupils when it started, to 130 on roll from September 2011. The largest group of pupils have been assessed as having severe learning difficulties (SLD), with a growing number with profound and multiple learning difficulties (PMLD) and another group who are on the autism spectrum.

 Case study: Sue Painter – Special school head teacher in Wales

The school has separate primary and secondary buildings, with a respite provision on the same site. This is run by Social Services, but with very close links to the school. The special school is co-located with an adjacent secondary school, where it has a transition class. Integration has always been part of what the school does and nearly a third of the pupils spend some time in mainstream classes with the support of the secondary school head teacher and his staff.

A recent development has been to have a satellite provision for children who need to have access to the Welsh medium. This is at a mixed 11–18 comprehensive school of nearly 1200 pupils, which is 24 miles away. Because of the distance between the two schools, the heads have an understanding that the day-to-day responsibility will be in the hands of the

(Continued)

(Continued)

mainstream head teacher. The children in the bilingual provision are mostly children who were borderline for coming into a special school.

The CLDD Research Project

At one of the project schools, the two teachers with classes for PMLD pupils each identified one pupil where there was concern about how little progress the child was making. One was a 15-year-old girl with Down's syndrome, hearing impairment and a range of other problems. The other was a 13-year-old boy who is a wheelchair user and has some visual impairment, epilepsy, a chromosome abnormality and other difficulties. Despite the extra time commitment that arose from being part of the pilot, both teachers were pleased with the lasting impact the approach has had on both children. Other pupils are now benefiting from the approach and the wider staff team is becoming familiar with the materials.

In the case of the girl, she is a child who has always been extremely passive, never initiated activities or made choices. Through using the Engagement Profile, her teacher was able to find activities that appealed to her and through which she came to realise that she could influence her environment and take the lead in engaging with staff. In the case of the boy, who had previously only enjoyed self-directed tactile experiences, he learnt to make eye contact, to accept new experiences offered by the staff and to participate in a wider range of activities. The Engagement Scale indicated that both had made noticeable progress during the time of the project.

Sue's leadership team includes a deputy head, an assistant head, a senior teacher, a senior LSA, the site manager and a governor. The school council, which has a slot at each of the main governing body meetings, sometimes presents the case for an improvement they want to see, such as a sixth-form common room. They also approached the local council about making it easier for pupils in wheelchairs to visit the local supermarket, whereby the council was persuaded to lower the kerb and to add a pedestrian crossing.

Sue's leadership style is to be open, receptive to new ideas, and to communicate everything as soon as possible via an e-portal. She says: 'I don't hide anything; everything is upfront.' She has a staff body who, she says, challenge each other, trust each other and look together for ways of moving forward. Sue says: 'They will take ideas on board, think about them, discuss, negotiate, and then, if everyone is agreed, they will work hard together to make it happen.'

Today's leaders

Increasingly, recognition has been given to the fact that, in a sense, all staff in a school are required at times to lead, whether as class or subject teachers, heads of department or key stage coordinators, or as part of senior management or leadership teams.

At can be seen from the case studies, there are endless permutations for how schools are organised, depending on the type of school and the additional dimensions it has to its work. However, at the top, despite a very sensible and even necessary move to distribute leadership more widely, sits the head teacher or principal. As Christopher Day et al. point out in their book, *Leading Schools in Times of Change* (2000), there is a balance that has to be found between having a clear vision of how and where heads want to lead their schools, and giving staff the opportunity to express *their* ideas, which may sometimes point in a different direction. Ultimately, the balance of power lies with the head and governors, and by keeping lines of communication open and showing a willingness to listen, most staff will accept that this is the case.

School leaders have a major impact on the happiness of those they lead. If they use their power wisely, as most of them do, not only will it encourage staff and pupils to produce their best work, it will also ensure that when they are leading a change of direction, others will be more willing to follow. For, as Stoll and Fink mention in *Changing our Schools* (1996), leadership is not just about leaders; it is also about followers. The next chapter goes into more detail about the importance that needs to be given to the well-being of staff, as well as pupils, if schools are to be united by a common purpose.

Further reading

Day, C., Harris, A., Hadfield, M., Tolley, H. and Beresford, J. (2000) *Leading Schools in Times of Change*. Buckingham: Open University Press.
Goleman, D. (1996) *Emotional Intelligence: Why it can matter more than IQ*. London: Bloomsbury.
MacBeath, J. (1999) *Schools Must Speak for Themselves*. London: Routledge.
Stoll, L. and Fink, D. (1996) *Changing our Schools*. Buckingham: Open University Press.

Useful website

http://complexld.ssatrust.org.uk

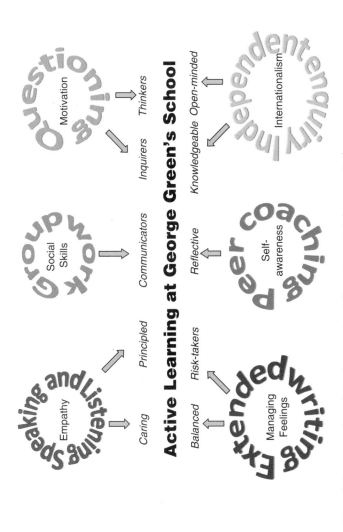

Active Learning at George Green's School

Figure 4.1   George Green's School's intepretation of the International Baccalaureate's learner attributes

Photocopiable:

How Successful Schools Work © Rona Tutt and Paul Williams, 2012

In **Summer Term One** we are working around the theme of **Managing Feelings,** using **extended writing** to help us become more balanced and better risk-takers.

Balanced *learners understand the importance of intellectual, physical and emotional balance to achieve personal well-being for themselves and others.* ***Risk-takers*** *approach unfamiliar situations and uncertainty with courage and forethought, and have the independence of spirit to explore new roles, ideas and strategies. They are brave and articulate in defending their beliefs.*

Learners are aiming to:

- Express their emotions clearly and openly to others and in ways appropriate to situations.
- Understand that how they express their feelings can have a significant impact both on other people and what happens to them.
- Have a range of strategies for managing impulses and strong emotions so they do not lead them to behave in negative ways.
- Anticipate, take and manage risks.
- Be confident in discussing controversial issues.
- Know what makes themselves feel good and know how to have a good time in ways that are not damaging to themselves or others.
- Manage their emotions, and build and maintain relationships.
- Deal with competing pressures, including personal and work-related demands.
- Understand how health can be affected by emotions and know a range of ways to keep themselves well and happy.
- Have a range of strategies to reduce, manage or change strong and uncomfortable feelings such as anger, anxiety, stress and jealousy.

Figure 4.2   Summer term 1

Photocopiable:

How Successful Schools Work © Rona Tutt and Paul Williams, 2012

In **Summer Term Two** we are working around the theme of **Internationalism**, using **independent inquiry** to help us become more **knowledgeable** and **open-minded.**

Knowledgeable learners explore concepts, ideas and issues that have local and global significance. In so doing, they acquire in-depth knowledge and develop understanding across a broad and balanced range of disciplines. *Open-minded* learners understand and appreciate their own cultures and personal histories, and are open to the perspectives, values and traditions of other individuals and communities. They are accustomed to seeking and evaluating a range of points of view, and are willing to grow from the experience.

Learners are aiming to:

- Generate ideas and explore possibilities.
- Identify questions to answer and problems to resolve.
- Connect their own and others' ideas and experiences in inventive ways.
- Analyse and evaluate information, judging its relevance and value.
- Support conclusions, using reasoned arguments and evidence.
- Explore, enjoy and celebrate the UK's increasing diversity.
- Promote the school's vision of a diverse, inclusive, tolerant and equitable society.

AFL spotlight on:
Independent learning

Figure 4.3   Summer term 2

Photocopiable:

How Successful Schools Work © Rona Tutt and Paul Williams, 2012

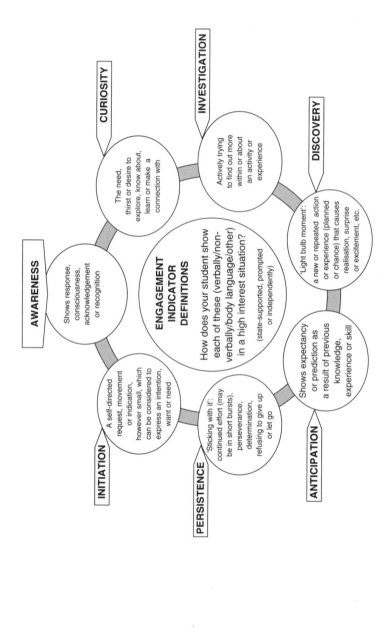

ENGAGEMENT INDICATOR DEFINITIONS

How does your student show each of these (verbally/non-verbally/body language/other) in a high interest situation?

(state-supported, prompted or independently)

CURIOSITY
The need, thirst or desire to explore, know about, learn or make a connection with

INVESTIGATION
Actively trying to find out more within or about an activity or experience

DISCOVERY
'Light bulb moment': a new or repeated action or experience (planned or chance) that causes realisation, surprise or excitement, etc.

AWARENESS
Shows response, consciousness, acknowledgement or recognition

INITIATION
A self-directed request, movement or indication, however small, which can be considered to express an intention, want or need

PERSISTENCE
'Sticking with it': continued effort (may be in short bursts), perseverance, determination, refusing to give up or let go

ANTICIPATION
Shows expectancy or prediction as a result of previous knowledge, experience or skill

Figure 4.4   Engagement Indicator Profile © B. Carpenter et al., 2011

Photocopiable:

How Successful Schools Work © Rona Tutt and Paul Williams, 2012

Engagement Indicators Chart and Scale © B. Carpenter et al., 2011

Student name:

Lesson/activity:

Date:

Date for review:

Age:

Target:

Time:

Completed by:

Overview of relevant issues

e.g. environment/learner mood/noteworthy factors or differences

What 'next action' are you using from the last scale you completed?

e.g. introduce a computer-based initial activity to reduce demands on student when s/he first arrives at lesson; explain individually to student before lesson what s/he will be doing

ENGAGEMENT SCALE

Mark TOTAL engagement score from sheet overleaf:

No focus		Emerging/ fleeting								Partly sustained							Mostly sustained							Fully sustained			
0	1	2	3	4	5	6	7	8	9	10	11	12	13	14	15	16	17	18	19	20	21	22	23	24	25	26	27	28

(Continued)

(Continued)

Engagement Indicators	Score (0–4)	What happened? What happened? What didn't happen and why?	Next actions What will I do next time and why? How will I make the activity more appealing (see Inquiry Framework)?
Responsiveness			
Curiosity			
Investigation			
Discovery			
Anticipation			
Initiation			
Persistence			
Total score		NB NOW CIRCLE TOTAL SCORE ON SCALE (previous page)	

Key for scoring	0	1	2	3	4
	No focus	Low and minimal levels – emerging/fleeting	Partly sustained	Mostly sustained	Fully sustained

Figure 4.5   Engagement Indicators Chart and Scale © B. Carpenter et al., 2011

 Photocopiable:

5

Generating well-being

> **Chapter overview**
>
> In this chapter, it is argued that a commitment to the well-being of both staff and pupils lies at the heart of successful school leadership.
>
> There is an explanation of how this became of interest to governments, for example through the SEAL (social and emotional aspects of learning) programme, and examples are given of schools where well-being is felt to be a defining characteristic.
>
> The impact of the environment is also considered in terms of the effect it has on the well-being of pupils and staff. This includes both indoor and outdoor learning.

Definitions

There are many definitions of what well-being encompasses. Some people see it as being mainly to do with health-related activities, while for others it will be about having time to be with family and friends, or indulging in enjoyable leisure activities. Others may treat the whole concept with a degree of cynicism. In terms of the school context, and as touched on towards the end of the previous chapter, the ideas and needs of individuals have to be balanced by school leaders with the needs of the organisation as a whole.

Well-being in the school context

Well-being as an important area of school life is getting an increasing amount of publicity. Working in a school can be an extremely stressful environment. Interacting with adults and large groups of children all day means that staff have to be both emotionally and physically resilient to all the demands that are made of them on a daily basis. How staff are managed and feel supported can make a real difference to what they and their students achieve and the two are closely linked.

The well-being of staff

Successful school leaders are those who make supporting their staff a priority and who recognise that it is as important for staff to look forward to going to school each day as it is for pupils to want to attend. In their book, *Winning the H Factor: The secrets of happy schools* (2010), Alistair Smith et al. describe the core elements of a happy school as: visible leadership, open communication, a focus on students and community cohesion, as well as good accommodation, charitable giving and staff events. They also add the need for good relationships with parents and the early resolution of conflicts. While initiative overload, unexpected events and unresolved conflicts can create additional stress, effective leaders will monitor the well-being of staff, conscious of the fact that: *Management is doing things right, leadership is doing the right things* (Drucker, 2001).

Well-being indicators for staff

Combining the information given so far with the views of school leaders, below are some indicators for the well-being of staff:

- feeling supported, heard and valued
- being encouraged to contribute ideas
- knowing it is acceptable to agree to disagree
- having clear lines of communication
- knowing problems can be shared rather than shelved
- feeling part of a team with no sense of 'them and us'
- enjoying the school environment and hearing laughter.

⌇ Questions for reflection

1   Do you agree with these indicators?
2   Do you feel anything is missing?
3   What would be your top three items?
4   How would you rate your own school in terms of the well-being of staff?

It is being suggested in this chapter that the well-being of staff is inextricably linked to the well-being of pupils, on the grounds that, if staff are under stress, it will be much harder for them to enthuse the pupils in front of them. Of course, few people live charmed lives and there will be times when personal worries or concerns will impact on the professional life of school staff. This is unavoidable, but what can be avoided is adding to the stress levels of staff by failing to recognise the importance of well-being and how it can be enhanced or undermined. School leaders, and indeed all staff, need to be watchful for signs of undue stress in their colleagues, as well as in themselves.

Activity

On the website below, try out the Pleasure and Well-Being Test. Whether or not you wish to submit your response, the questions are interesting in themselves.

www.attitudefactor.com – Click on 'Take first test' (5 mins)

The well-being of pupils

The introduction in 2003 of Every Child Matters (ECM) can be seen as a significant step in raising the status of pupils' well-being. The five ECM outcomes, devised with the help of children (being healthy, staying safe, enjoying and achieving, making a positive contribution, and achieving economic well-being) can all be seen as part of pupils' well-being.

SEAL – social and emotional aspects of learning

After the introduction of ECM and the Children Act that followed in 2004, a further impetus to support pupils' well-being came with the introduction of the SEAL programme, which was developed in 2005 by the National Strategies on behalf of the government. Originally designed for use in primary schools, the programme was sufficiently successful to be extended to secondary schools.

 Key points: SEAL – Social and emotional aspects of learning

The materials focus on five social and emotional aspects of learning, which are based on Goleman's (1996) model of the five domains of emotional intelligence (referred to in the previous chapter), namely:

- self-awareness
- managing feelings
- motivation
- empathy
- social skills.

Although support from the National Strategies is no longer available, schools have continued to use this, or a similar approach, to ensure that there is an emphasis on children's social and emotional development as well as their academic progress.

Schools are actively encouraged to explore different ways of implementing SEAL, meaning that they can tailor it to their own circumstances. In a sense, this means that SEAL is essentially what individual schools make of it.

Emotional resilience

In 2010, in an article entitled 'Building emotional resilience', Lucy Bailey pointed out that, according to the Institute of Psychiatry, the number of children in the UK with emotional and behavioural problems has doubled in the last 25 years, and the number of adolescent suicides has quadrupled. Her article goes on to outline the UK Resilience Programme (UKRP) and three areas – Hertfordshire, South Tyneside and Manchester – which were part of a well-being project that set out to improve happiness and well-being.

 Key points: UK Resilience Programme (UKRP)

The UK Resilience Programme is the UK's implementation of the Penn Resiliency Program developed at the University of Pennsylvania. It is based on 18 one-hour workshops, originally with the aim of preventing adolescent depression, but now with the broader remit of promoting:

- resilience and optimistic thinking
- adaptive coping skills
- problem solving.

This, in turn, aims to improve psychological well-being, and, potentially, behaviour, attendance and academic outcomes, by building resilience and changing thinking.

A three-year study by the London School of Economics (LSE) (DfE, 2011b) provided evidence that the programme was enjoyed by pupils and helped them to use the skills they had learned to modify their emotional responses. The programme was aimed at selected pupils in Year 7 and the majority of schools that took part were sufficiently impressed to extend it to all their Year 7 students.

Well-being indicators for pupils

In 2008, there was an Ofsted consultation on using well-being indicators as part of the inspection process. Inspectors suggested a list of what might be included, partly based on the five outcomes of ECM. Ofsted inspectors were looking for measures that were quantifiable and the concept of well-being does not necessarily lend itself to such an approach. The proposed indicators included the extent to which schools:

- promote healthy lifestyles and discourage the use of harmful substances
- help pupils to feel safe and discourage bullying
- ensure pupils can voice concerns and influence decisions
- help pupils to enjoy school and gain the knowledge and skills they need
- help pupils to manage their feelings and be resilient

- promote equality and counteract discrimination
- provide a good range of additional activities and opportunities to contribute to the local community.

The results of the consultation fed into the 2009 revision of the Ofsted framework. Since then, there has been a further revision and the framework, while concentrating on four key areas, continues to take account of the spiritual, moral, social and cultural development of pupils, as well as the extent to which the education provided enables every pupil to achieve her or his potential.

Values-based Education

As has already been suggested, a sense of well-being depends partly on making sure that people know they are valued and appreciate how to value others. This is sometimes referred to as Values Education or Values-based Education. A values-based school is one that has an educational philosophy which is based on valuing oneself, valuing others and caring for, or valuing, the environment. It recognises the worth of everyone involved in the life and work of the school community. It seeks to foster positive relationships and to help pupils gain self-respect, so that they are in a position to respect others. Adults act as good role models in helping pupils to become good citizens and effective learners.

Well-being in the context of Northern Ireland

This chapter has two case studies, from Northern Ireland, as children's well-being is a particular issue in divided communities with a history of conflict. In the example of a post-primary school, there is the added difficulty of raising self-esteem in a school where children have failed to get into the grammar school system. (Secondary schools in Northern Ireland are referred to as post-primary schools.)

Michael Newman's school opened in 1968 and has a capacity for 600. Falling rolls are creating some anxiety and are caused by the population on the housing estate having grown up and general demographic trends.

 Case study: Michael Newman – Principal of a Northern Ireland primary school

Michael Newman's school is a large primary school with a nursery unit. It has 516 children aged 3–11. Almost all the children go right through the school from the nursery onwards. The school has good links both with other primary and post-primary schools.

(Continued)

(Continued)

When he took over, there was a very large Senior Management Team (SMT), which Michael felt had grown too large, so he reformed it into a smaller, tighter team. His SLT consists of: the principal, the vice principal, the head of key stage 2, the head of nursery and the head of key stage 1. To help with succession planning, a representative from each key stage serves on the SLT in rotation, in order to gain experience. Next year, he plans to reorganise the team, so that there will be a core team (as above), plus a literacy and a numeracy coordinator as part of an extended team.

Michael has been influenced by Alistair Smith's Accelerated Learning approach, which fitted in with the school's link with the Comenius programme (run by the British Council to help schools develop international links). When he received a grant, he used it to give teachers time to talk to their year group partners and to try out ideas. He wanted to challenge the teachers about (i) their pedagogy and (ii) their interaction with pupils. As regards the latter, he says that occasionally heads come across teachers who never do develop a rapport with their pupils and, when this is the case, they are simply in the wrong profession.

Michael believes in tension-free discipline, which he describes as setting children clear boundaries and giving them an understanding of the consequences of making wrong choices, but within a context of considerable pastoral support. He sees pastoral care as being at the heart of the working ethos of the school, permeating all activities and decision making. As part of the curriculum, the school teaches a cross-curricular theme known as Personal Development and Mutual Understanding, which is designed to promote self-esteem, cooperation, tolerance and mutual respect. The school hosts a multi-agency support team (MAST), which provides speech therapy, occupational therapy, clinical psychology and behaviour management. Each year, the school carries out a pastoral audit as part of a holistic approach to health and well-being.

Michael says: 'You have to work within the community you serve and always think what benefits the children. You must have aspirations for them, because you can change their future. This means working with the parents, even if their own experience of school was poor.'

A post-primary school leader's approach

When he first arrived at the school, Andy McMorran's aim was to counteract a feeling of failure instilled in children who had not been successful in passing the 11+. He began by concentrating on literacy and numeracy and giving extra support to those who needed it. To improve staff well-being and motivation, Andy tackled a tendency for a 'them and us' culture between the staff and senior management, many of whom had been in post for a very long time and did not necessarily appreciate the need for change. He also felt that it was a very male-dominated atmosphere and so he appointed more women teachers. A section of the staff handbook is devoted to dealing with stress, and a confidential counselling service can be accessed by staff as well as students.

Case study: Andy McMorran – Principal of a boys' high school in Northern Ireland

The school has 650 boys aged 11–18. When Andy took over the school, he inherited a senior leadership team of seven. He increased this to 12 and made sure each member of the team was shadowed as part of succession planning. He encouraged all staff to express their opinions and to feel that what they had to offer was of merit. He also managed to keep class sizes down and introduced streaming, with the lowest stream having the highest levels of staffing. He raised the profile and the scope of the SEN department, funding staff salaries from non-stop fund-raising. Andy talks of the work of the SEN department as being vital to the school's success, as 40 per cent of the pupils are recognised as having SEN and about 30 per cent are statemented.

He has encouraged high aspirations and established a link with the University of Ulster so that A-level students can spend a day a week there on a bridging course. As a result, last year 36 out of 40 boys transferred to the university. Engineering has replaced woodwork and metalwork, while a Life and Works department and a Moving Image department have brought in a wider range of subjects and helped to motivate students. Previously, attendance had not been good, but since every absence or lateness has been followed up, very few parents have had to be contacted. The same approach is used with homework. Andy comments: 'As achievements have gone up, discipline problems have been reduced.'

As in the previous case study, some of the students take part in an Education for Mutual Understanding project aimed at developing their knowledge and understanding of cultural and religious diversity. The school has a strong pastoral support system that includes a school counsellor, who is easily accessible. Students can self-refer, as well as being referred through other channels when appropriate. The counsellor sees between 300 and 400 pupils a year.

Although nearing retirement, Andy says he is still enthused by his role as principal and talks of 'the importance of maintaining an optimistic demeanour, regardless of what hits you', a sentiment that will be echoed by many school leaders.

Another aspect of well-being may be seen as the absence of conflict. An approach that originated in the criminal justice system, but which is becoming increasingly used in schools and other settings is 'restorative justice'.

Restorative justice

This approach was first mentioned in this book in relation to the case study of Anne McCormick and her school in Chapter 4, where she found it was relevant to helping even very young children understand the effect that wrong actions can have on others. Andrew Sleeth, who was mentioned in Chapter 3 for his efforts in integrating different communities, has found that the restorative justice approach helps to avoid conflict between all stakeholders.

After learning about this approach, he trialled its use with students, without advertising the fact. After being convinced of its value, he managed to obtain a grant so that he had the money to train staff, pupils, parents and governors, which helped them to change their mindset. In this approach, which is a way of bringing victims and offenders together, everyone has a chance to be heard, no one is judged and conflicts are resolved in a non-judgemental way.

 Key points: Restorative justice

This practice has been adopted from the criminal justice system, giving victims of crime the opportunity to explain to the perpetrators the effect on them that the crime has had. It enables them to question the offender and seek some answers as to why they behaved as they did, while letting the offender gain an insight into the impact of their actions on others. The approach has four key features:

- respect – listening to others and valuing their opinions
- responsibility – taking responsibility for one's actions
- repair – developing the skills to help repair harm, find solutions and try to prevent any repetition
- reintegration – working through a structured process that solves problems and reintegrates the offender into the school community.

The four key questions are:

1 What has happened?
2 Who has been affected? In what way?
3 How can we involve everyone who has been affected to find a way forward?
4 What do you think needs to happen to make things right?

The next case study is of a head teacher and her staff who go the extra mile to boost the well-being of students and their families in an area where many would otherwise lead very restricted lives.

Well-being in a London secondary school

Jo Shuter is the head teacher in the next case study, which is about a school where a sense of family and well-being permeates all aspects of the school's work.

Case study: Jo Shuter – Head teacher of a London community foundation school

The school has 1430 students aged 11–19, in an area that has pockets of extreme deprivation: 52 per cent of the students are entitled to free school meals (FSM); 40 per cent of the pupils have SEND; and, for many, English is their third or fourth language. The school gained specialist status for technology in 2001, foundation status in 2008 and, as Jo is a National Leader of Education (NLE), her school is a National Support School (NSS). Its work as a full service extended school is an integral part of what it does to support students and their families.

The more able pupils aim for the English Baccalaureate (EBacc) and can follow a range of GCSE and BTEC courses. A similar range of A-levels and BTECs are available to A-level students, who will be aiming to go to university. For other students, their needs dictate the courses they follow, including working on the school's farm, where some of the more vulnerable pupils benefit from being able to nurture the goats, chickens, guinea pigs and other animals. This can lead to a BTEC in Land Studies (equal to two GCSEs). Others study horticulture, growing vegetables and learning to arrange floral displays.

Breakfast is heavily subsidised and open to primary schools. The onsite youth club has 200 children a night, which helps to keep them off the streets and gives them something constructive to do. They are supported by NQTs who are teaching at the school and who are paid extra for helping one evening each week. This broadens their experience and helps them to build relationships with the students. Everyone is involved in INSET days, including office staff, kitchen staff and site staff, so that there is a consistent message given to the students.

Well-being programmes include 52 support staff, youth workers, farm workers, counsellors, art, drama and music therapists, family therapists, psychotherapists and access to cognitive behaviour therapy (CBT). There have been no permanent exclusions for the last three years and attendance rates have gone up to 96 per cent. There is a strong emphasis on student voice. Each of the seven areas – prefects, school council, inclusion voice, assistant youth workers, peer mentors, student action group and strategic student voice – are led by a student, who, between them, form the Student Leadership Board.

The school has a business arm. Places are sold on its vocational courses and in its alternative provision known as ASPIRE (standing for 'aspire to learn'), which has separate provision for key stage 3 and key stage 4 pupils. There is offsite provision for key stage 5 NEETs (those who are Not in Education, Employment or Training) from across the borough, but run by the school. Here, the focus is on 'ASPIRE to work'. There is a café onsite for staff, visitors and sixth-formers, which helps to subsidise other catering.

A recent development is to set up a registered charity to try to raise enough money to acquire a house for sixth-form students who are made homeless, so that they are able to concentrate on their studies in an appropriate environment. The University of Westminster has agreed that they can have student accommodation in the holidays, after which the school will help to settle them into flats. Jo says: 'We do whatever it takes to climb over barriers and work with pupils and their families. We never give up on any child, which is why so many of them return and join the staff.'

The impact of the environment

The environment in which people work is known to affect how they feel. In recent years, there has been a growing recognition of the importance of the educational environment and the effect it has on learners. Since the 1990s, a variety of building programmes have taken place, some of which have relied heavily on public–private partnership (PPP) arrangements, including the private finance initiative (PFI), which helped fund Building Schools for the Future (BSF). Although this ambitious programme has been cancelled, all these developments generated some exciting school buildings and reflect the wider role that schools are expected to play at the heart of their communities.

The outdoor curriculum

Schools of all sizes are paying more attention to outdoor learning, with playgrounds on roof tops, imaginative play areas, and animals and plants adding to the scope of the curriculum. The final case study in this chapter shows how the indoor and outdoor environments can be brought together in an unusual way.

Mark Cole runs a children's centre in a London borough. He has developed a unique environment in which young children can learn through being outside and very active for much of the time. The unusual design was created to brighten up a rather drab estate, which is in the process of regeneration.

 Case study: Mark Cole – Head teacher of a children's centre in north-west London

Contained within an award-winning design, which uses three-storey sea containers and a Mongolian Yurt, and where there is total integration of the outdoor and indoor areas, with only mesh walls to the outside, the children's centre houses under one roof:

- a phase 1 children's centre, delivering the full service model from 8am to 6pm
- a nursery school

(Continued)

(Continued)

- provision for 10 places for 2–4-year-olds with a diagnosis of autism
- the borough's advisory service for children and young people up to 19 years of age with autism.

In addition, the children's centre is a hub for training and supporting childminders; encourages parents and carers to become involved, to meet together and to make their views known; and gives them access to other services.

The children have a great deal of choice in where they want to go within this safe and very varied environment. Everywhere, there are different areas to explore and a range of activities to stir their imagination and to encourage them to play together. If they feel cold, the Yurt or the inside areas provide warmth and a further set of activities.

When he arrived three years ago, the head teacher, Mark, concentrated on uniting the children's centre and the nursery and putting in place a leadership team that would go across the provision. Now that this has been accomplished, he feels that his role is to be a leader of leaders and a physical presence rather than being hands-on. The work he has put into creating this environment has enabled his centre to form a partnership with a neighbouring children's centre, which he and his team have been asked to run, as well as federating with a neighbouring nursery school and children's centre. This will mean that he and his leadership team will have responsibility for two schools on three sites.

He is keen on creating a centre for leaders and he has made sure that training at all levels has been made available to staff. Team building supports this work. He uses the National College to support staff development and his aim is to drive forward sustained, incremental improvement. (Copies of the organisational structure and team pledges are given at the end of the chapter in Figures 5.1 and 5.2.)

Taking on these extra responsibilities has happened very recently and Mark is confident that he and his leadership team have the capacity and experience to expand their roles in this way. He says: 'At present, we are working on the structures that need to be in place and creating shared visions, together with a common set of values across the partnership.'

So, while the pace of change remains as frantic as ever, and while the promised cut-back in bureaucracy and red tape is still in its infancy, school leaders need to be aware of the need to look after themselves, in order to be able to look after their staff and their pupils. As no one is likely to invent more hours in the day, it is up to school leaders to keep themselves healthy and fit, so that they can create an environment where the well-being of all is treated as a priority.

Further reading

Department for Children, Schools and Families (DCSF) (2007a) *Social and Emotional Aspects of Learning for Secondary Schools.* Nottingham: DCSF Publications.

Department for Education (DfE) (2011b) *UK Resilience Programme Evaluation: Final report*. Available at: www.education.gov.uk/publications

Drucker, P. (2001) *The Essential Drucker: The best of sixty years of Peter Drucker's essential writings on management*. New York: Harper Books.

Smith, A. with Jones, J. and Reid, J. (2010) *Winning the H Factor: The secrets of happy schools*. London: Continuum.

Useful website

www.attitudefactor.com

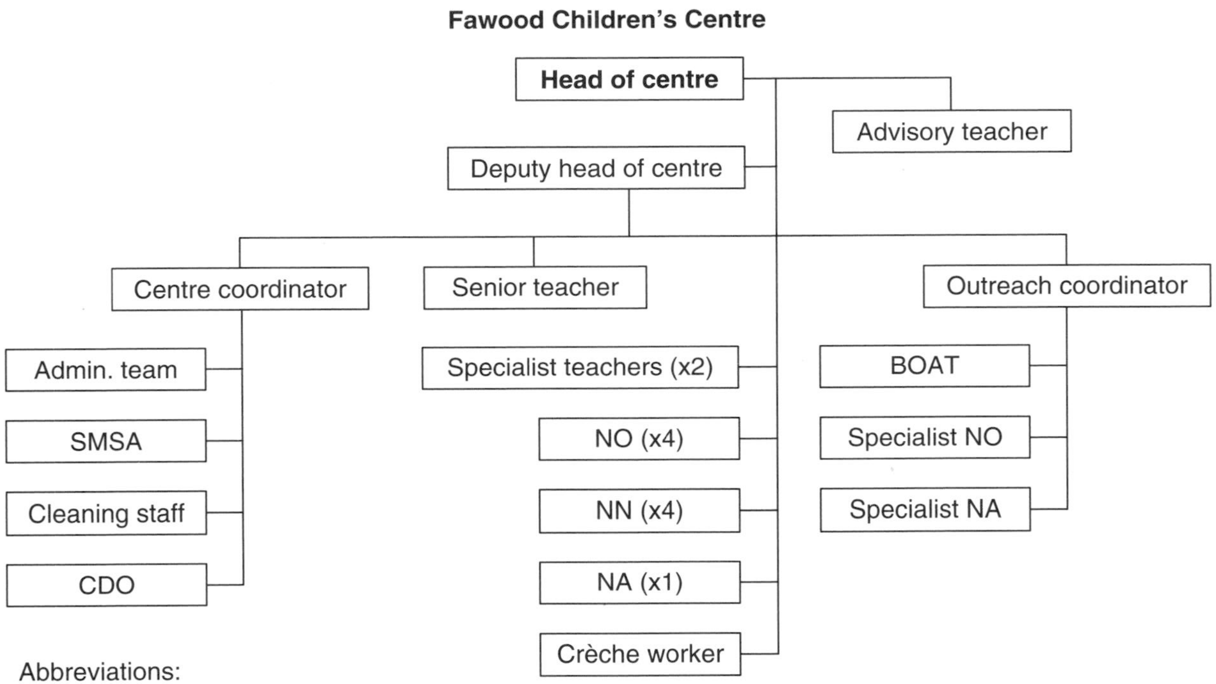

Fawood Children's Centre

```
                                    Head of centre ──────── Advisory teacher
                                          │
          ┌───────────────────────────────┼───────────────────────────────┐
          │                               │                                │
   Centre coordinator            Deputy head of centre            Outreach coordinator
          │                               │                                │
  ┌───┬───┼───┬───┐          ┌────────────┼──────┬──────┬──────┐      ┌─────┼────────┐
  │   │   │   │              │            │      │      │      │      │     │        │
Admin.  SMSA  Cleaning  CDO  Senior  Specialist  NO    NN     NA   Crèche BOAT Specialist  Specialist
team          staff          teacher teachers   (x4)  (x4)   (x1)  worker       NO          NA
                                     (x2)
```

Abbreviations:

BOAT – Brent Outreach Autism Team
CDO – Community development officer
NA   – Nursery assistant
NN   – Nursery nurse
NO   – Nursery officer
SMSA – School meals supervisor assistant

Figure 5.1   Organisational structure

Photocopiable:

How Successful Schools Work © Rona Tutt and Paul Williams, 2012

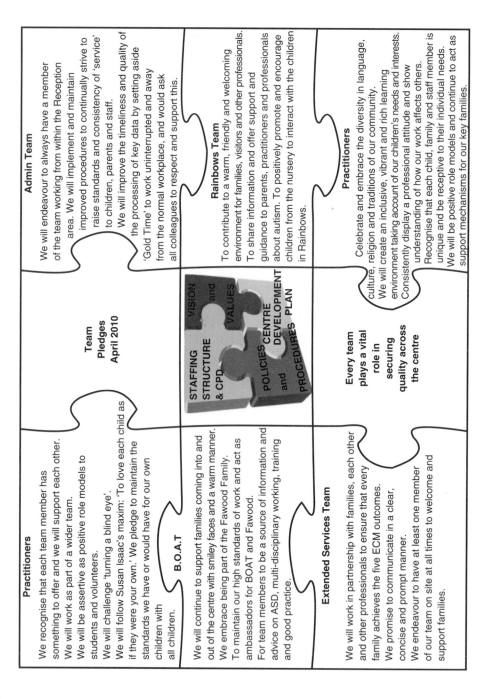

Practitioners

We recognise that each team member has something to offer and we will support each other.

We will work as part of a wider team.

We will be assertive as positive role models to students and volunteers.

We will challenge 'turning a blind eye'.

We will follow Susan Isaac's maxim: 'To love each child as if they were your own.' We pledge to maintain the standards we have or would have for our own children with all children.

B.O.A.T

We will continue to support families coming into and out of the centre with smiley faces and a warm manner. We embrace being part of the Fawood Family.

To maintain our high standards of work and act as ambassadors for BOAT and Fawood.

For team members to be a source of information and advice on ASD, multi-disciplinary working, training and good practice.

Extended Services Team

We will work in partnership with families, each other and other professionals to ensure that every family achieves the five ECM outcomes.

We promise to communicate in a clear, concise and prompt manner.

We endeavour to have at least one member of our team on site at all times to welcome and support families.

Team Pledges April 2010

STAFFING STRUCTURE & CPD

VISION and VALUES

POLICIES and PROCEDURES

CENTRE DEVELOPMENT PLAN

Every team plays a vital role in securing quality across the centre

Admin Team

We will endeavour to always have a member of the team working from within the Reception area. We will implement and maintain improved procedures to continually strive to raise standards and consistency of 'service' to children, parents and staff.

We will improve the timeliness and quality of the processing of key data by setting aside 'Gold Time' to work uninterrupted and away from the normal workplace, and would ask all colleagues to respect and support this.

Rainbows Team

To contribute to a warm, friendly and welcoming environment for families, visitors and other professionals. To share information and offer support and guidance to parents, practitioners and professionals about autism. To positively promote and encourage children from the nursery to interact with the children in Rainbows.

Practitioners

Celebrate and embrace the diversity in language, culture, religion and traditions of our community.

We will create an inclusive, vibrant and rich learning environment taking account of our children's needs and interests. Consistently display a professional attitude and show understanding of how our work affects others.

Recognise that each child, family and staff member is unique and be receptive to their individual needs.

We will be positive role models and continue to act as support mechanisms for our key families.

Figure 5.2   Team pledges

Photocopiable:

Staying at the forefront

> **Chapter overview**
>
> This chapter looks at how school leaders manage to keep at the forefront of educational changes by taking advantage of emerging possibilities, such as being more involved in initial teacher training (ITT) and continuing professional development (CPD), or making better use of technology.
>
> The final case study in the book is about one of the pilot schools for Achievement for All (AfA), an approach to raising standards that the government hopes will be of interest to all schools.
>
> The chapter ends with a mention of schools becoming engaged with the idea of sustainable leadership.

With change being so rapid, there is a need for school leaders to continually update their own knowledge, as well as making sure that their staff are developing in a way that enables the school to move forward. It is a mark of innovative and successful school leaders that they not only adjust to altered situations, but are able to be proactive in planning ahead for their school or schools.

As mentioned in the opening chapter, the National College for School Leadership (NCSL) was established to ensure that school leaders and those aspiring to become school leaders would have access to high quality training. In March 2012, the NCSL became an Executive Agency within the DfE, but continues to be responsible for both the NPQH (National Professional Qualification for Headship) and the NPQICL (National Professional Qualification in Integrated Centre Leadership) for those working in children's centres and other integrated settings. As mentioned in the Introduction, the DfE has announced that the NPQH is likely to become non-mandatory, while the NPQICL was refreshed during 2011/12.

General training

The National Scholarship Fund for Teachers was announced in the White Paper, *The Importance of Teaching* (DfE, 2010c), and launched in June 2011.

It is open to people with qualified teacher status (QTS) who work in schools funded by the government, and who want to study at Masters level. While the previous government was keen for teachers to pursue the Masters in Teaching and Learning (MTL), the present government argues that teachers should be free to choose their own courses at this level.

SEND training

As mentioned in Chapter 3, there has been an increase in the training opportunities to address the needs of pupils with special educational needs and disabilities (SEND). In 2011, the National Association for Special Education Needs (nasen) was given funding by the DfE to put together a SEND toolkit for every school. Around 25 lead SENCOs are responsible for training regional clusters of SENCOs, as a way of ensuring that staff in every school can receive a basic level of training in SEND.

A further source of information and training in specific areas of SEND are the three trusts which were set up by the government in 2008:

- **The Autism Education Trust** has developed three levels of training in autism education: whole-school training; training for staff working regularly with children and young people on the autism spectrum; and specialist training aimed at SENCOs and others who want to gain specialist knowledge in this area. This training became available from March 2012.
- **The Communication Trust** aims to highlight the importance of speech, language and communication across the children's workforce and to make sure that practitioners have access to the best training and expertise available in the field.
- **The Dyslexia-SpLD Trust (DST)** helped to establish the training for the 4000 specialist teachers of dyslexia recommended by the Rose Review (which was mentioned in Chapter 3).

 Activity

Go to one or more of these websites and see what they have to offer:

- www.autismeducationtrust.org.uk – the page on Training Hubs gives further information on the tiers of training and how it is organised.
- www.thecommunicationtrust.org.uk – click on Programme of Work and investigate the training and material available for early years, primary years or secondary years.
- www.thedyslexia-spldtrust.org.uk – under Our Work, see the plans for 2011–13 and news of the Trust's professional development framework.

Not all training is costly. Some may be delivered by *blended learning* (a mixture of face-to-face and online training) and others are free to download. This includes the Inclusion Development Programme (IDP) which was mentioned in Chapter 3, materials on the Trusts' websites and several on the TDA's own website. Online modules, developed in the wake of the complex learning difficulties and disabilities (CLDD) project mentioned in Chapter 4, became available in 2012.

Teaching schools

In the past, some schools have been training schools. In its White Paper, *The Importance of Teaching*, the government outlined its plans for teaching schools. The designation is open to any phase or type of school, as well as sixth-form colleges, pupil referral units (PRUs), independent schools and academies (including free schools).

 Key points: Training schools and teaching schools

Training schools – this was a programme run by the TDA, under which 242 schools were designated centres of excellence in training and development. Their purpose was to help deliver high quality initial teacher training (ITT) and professional development.

Teaching schools – the aim is to create a national network of 500 schools which will be involved in ITT in their area, in conjunction with universities, and with CPD. As well as helping to supply new teachers, teaching schools will help to develop the school leaders of the future.

The first tranche of successful schools were announced in July 2011 and given a year to plan for taking on this considerable commitment. To be eligible, schools must be judged outstanding by Ofsted, and have a track record of being involved in ITT, leadership development and school improvement. Each teaching school is responsible for leading a group of schools, known as an alliance. Some of the schools within the alliance will be strategic partners, who will support the teaching school by carrying out elements of its role. Other strategic partners can be LAs, diocesan bodies or private companies. Teaching schools must be linked to at least one university and will receive core funding for four years. They can generate extra income through some of the courses and other services they deliver.

Steve Munby, the chief executive of the NCSL, is quoted in a DfE news and press release notice (24 November 2010) as saying: 'The expansion of our National and Local Leaders of Education programmes; the roll-out of teaching schools and the designation of specialist leaders of education will change the face of education in this country forever.'

The first teaching schools

The first 100 teaching schools (36 primary, 57 secondary and 7 special schools) began operating in September 2011, with the next 100 being announced in spring 2012. One of the successful secondary schools is part of the federation under Dame Yasmin Bevan, which was provided as a case study in Chapter 2. One of the first special schools to be designated is a school in the south west, where the head teacher, David Gregory, spent many years teaching in mainstream schools before moving into special education. His school is very much involved with the local community, including local schools, and, for many years, he has worked closely with mainstream schools to share expertise and professional development. He has also worked with the NCSL to deliver courses on leadership, which he sees as generic, cutting across different phases and sectors.

 Case study: David Gregory – Head of one of the first teaching schools

David's school caters for 170 pupils aged 3 to 19 with a wide range of needs: 70 per cent are on the autism spectrum, including a small group who have Asperger's syndrome and are taught mainly in a satellite class at a local secondary school. There are places for 12 pupils to be residential on a weekly basis. As part of Project Search, post-16 students can spend up to a year at a large city hospital, where the school has a classroom, staffed by a teacher and teaching assistant from David's school. For much of each day, however, they are working in various departments as interns, supported by job development advisers. As a result of this scheme, the majority of participating students have obtained employment, either at the hospital or with other companies.

The school, which is a specialist technology college, aims to offer much more than the national curriculum. There is a café, which is open to parents, families and to the general public, as well as a wide range of after-school and holiday-time activities. David believes in giving his pupils the emotional ability to cope with the challenges the outside world brings and hopes that the school has a lifelong relationship with them.

The school is already a trust foundation school and is waiting to hear the result of its application for academy status. David says that the decision to go for academy status was a natural consequence of considering the national context (the macro environment), the future of the school (the micro environment) and the future educational landscape. He sees it as helping to raise the students' aspirations for adult life. He is keen to offer more opportunities at post-16 and post-19 as well. He believes that far more pupils with learning difficulties than at present, are capable of holding down a job and says: 'We want to engage with families and children to raise aspirations for their adult life, not just for the end of their schooling.' He expects the relationship between school and the local authority to be a collaborative one and to remain very important.

(Continued)

(Continued)

David describes the move to become a teaching school as a natural development of the work he already does with mainstream schools, including taking ITT students for placement blocks and having links with Graduate Teacher Programme (GTP) consortia. He put in a joint bid with a school for SLD/PMLD pupils, so that between them, they can cover most aspects of SEND. Although they will be combining to deliver some of the training, they are linked to different universities and David is concentrating on working with mainstream primary and secondary schools. Both schools are keen to influence the content of ITT courses, so that trainee teachers are better equipped to deal with the wide range of needs and abilities to be found in most of today's classrooms.

In the past, special schools have sometimes been seen as a last resort. David says he wants his school 'to be parents' first choice of school for their child, not as the consequence of being referred'.

 Activity

Go to the NCSL's website (www.nationalcollege.org.uk) and look at the information on teaching schools, including:

- the five-minute self assessment tool for measuring your eligibility to become a teaching school
- the national teaching schools' prospectus.

Another leading provider of professional development for school leaders is The Schools Network (previously the Specialist Schools and Academies Trust [SSAT]), whose slogan is: *By schools for schools*. Its aim is to transform education through providing practical support to schools by having a network of innovative, high performing schools and academies, as well as working in partnership with businesses and the wider community.

Leadership and innovation hubs

These were established by The Schools Network in response to schools saying they wanted leadership programmes delivered locally by leading head teachers and practitioners. The first hub schools were established in September 2010. The first special school that acted as a pilot for the project was Penny Barratt's school in London. Already well established for its training programme to local schools, Penny said the move to become a hub school was a natural progression of their CPD work.

Case study: Penny Barratt – Leadership and innovation hub school, London

Penny's school grew out of a merger between an SLD/PMLD school on two sites, plus a separate school for pupils with autism. It moved to its current sites in 2007, with the primary department being co-located with a primary school and the secondary department being co-located with a secondary school. There are over 150 pupils aged 2–19 at the school, divided equally between the two sites.

Some of the more able children, particularly those on the autism spectrum, have access to a class at the primary school, where they have opportunities to follow a more mainstream curriculum and to integrate into other classes for some of their lessons. The secondary department is joined to the secondary school by a new sports centre, to which both sets of pupils have access.

The school has a long tradition of working with other schools, along with a strong training and research focus. It runs an ASD outreach team for the Borough, offers a training and consultancy service, and is a National Support School (NSS), working intensively with two other schools. The head views their work as an NSS as a great development opportunity for her staff, as well as supporting the schools concerned. As part of the changes brought about by the move from three sites to two and the change in status to a hub school, the head has restructured the leadership team (see Figure 6.1). She is not keen on the title of 'head teacher', as she says her two deputies are in charge of the day-to-day running of the primary and secondary departments, and that her role goes far beyond traditional boundaries. The larger and more complex the school has become, the more it has needed to be run on business lines, but a business that is focused on learning. She is hoping that the Managed Learning Environment (MLE) will help in this direction.

Penny says that the main difference in the way they run courses as a hub school is that they find out what the local schools want and then provide it, rather than putting on the courses they think other schools need. They have tried to run courses for mainstream and special schools together, but Penny is thinking of splitting these in order to make them more focused on the schools' needs.

Penny says her view of the future would be to have the school open for 48 weeks a year, from 8am to 6pm and for six or seven days a week. As with the current elements of the school's work, she would want to establish the provisions that would be necessary, but then hand them over to others to run, once the standards have been set. She describes being a head teacher in the current climate as positioning yourself so that you can take advantage of new developments: 'You have your foot in lots of doors, so that you can seize your opportunity as each door opens.'

Technological advances

It would be wrong not to mention some of the technological advances that schools are now using, both to enhance pupils' learning and to help run the increasingly complex world of schools. After Virtual Learning Environments became well known, around the turn of the century, the term *Managed Learning Environments* (MLEs) came into being. There is not always complete agreement about the definition of MLEs, *Virtual Learning Environments* (VLEs) and the more general term of *Learning Platforms*.

Key points: Technological terms

Managed Learning Environment (MLE)

This is an integrated learning management system that offers a range of tools for online learning and collaboration. The focus is on making it easier to manage the learning process, by joining up several separate systems.

Virtual Learning Environment (VLE)

In contrast to MLEs, VLEs are computer programs that are designed to support teaching and e-learning. VLEs usually work over the internet and can be used to make learning more interactive and to create blended learning.

Learning Platforms

The term is sometimes used to cover both MLEs and VLEs, as it describes a broad range of ICT systems that are used to deliver and support learning, by bringing together hardware, software and supporting services, with personalised online space for every pupil.

One school that has ICT firmly embedded in teaching and learning is an inner London primary school, where the head teacher, Jeff Smith, sees technology as a way of giving children access to a broader perspective, which, in a school where 37 languages are used by the children, is one way of helping them to feel part of a close-knit school community as well as the global community. The head teacher describes it as *a doorway out of the four walls of the building*. The school has an MLE and has no difficulty in attracting teaching and support staff through its striking video advertisements on the school's website. Getting hold of staff in this way also helps to ensure that only those who have an interest in ICT are likely to apply.

Case study: Jeff Smith – Head teacher of an inner-city primary school

The school has 400 pupils aged 3–11, who, between them, speak 37 different languages. In addition, they all learn Spanish from the age of 7, a language that was selected partly because it is no child's first language, so it creates a level playing field. The school does not seek to iron out the differences between pupils from a very wide range of backgrounds, languages and cultures, but to provide a curriculum that is broad enough to embrace difference.

The head teacher believes in a flat management structure and in encouraging staff development at all levels. Several staff have attended the National College's 'Leading from the Middle' course. Having turned the school around from a school that was not doing very well to one that is oversubscribed, and having a stable leadership team, he encourages others to take the lead in coming forward with ideas while he and his deputy act as facilitators in seeing them through.

The school is one of 10 Microsoft Partner schools, which link with each other, have online discussion forums and run courses both here and abroad. All children have their own laptop from the age of 7 and soon become adept at integrating information from the web into their work. As part of the school's approach to e-safety, the children are taught about social networking and create their own page, so that they can learn about what it is appropriate to put on and will know how to use Facebook later on.

By the age of 9, they are creating their own PowerPoint presentations. Much of this work encourages working in pairs and small groups as well as on their own. The pupils are responsible for running the school's radio station, which is housed in a fully equipped studio. At break times, they have the opportunity to use the bank of monitors on display in a wide corridor area, where they can exercise using a selection of computer games, with movement sensor controls. There is no need for a computer suite, as technology is wired into every classroom and the children have ready access to their individual laptops when they need them.

Jeff has had two headships and has thought about moving on to a larger school, but has decided that he would prefer to continue to move his present school forward. Making full use of the MLE will be the next stage of the school's technological advances.

Whereas Jeff worked with Microsoft to make sure that his school is well equipped to give pupils the skills they need, a number of other schools have offered to trial new methods, materials or ways of working. This is a useful way of keeping at the forefront of developments. The final case study in this book is a school that helped to pilot *Achievement for All*.

Achievement for All (AfA)

AfA is a whole-school approach to school improvement, with a particular focus on the 20 per cent of vulnerable learners including SEND pupils.

It was piloted in 450 primary, secondary and special schools across 10 local authorities between 2009 and 2011 (DCSF, 2009a). In the Green Paper, *Support and Aspiration: A new approach to SEND* (DfE, 2011a), the current government expressed its intention of taking forward this approach with a view to making it available to schools across the country.

 Key points: Achievement for All (AfA)

The aims of AfA are three-fold:

- to improve the achievement and progress of children and young people, with a particular focus on the 20 per cent of vulnerable learners including SEND pupils
- to improve engagement with their parents
- to improve wider outcomes, i.e. prevent bullying and increase attendance.

The three-pronged approach to achieving these aims is through:

1 Assessment, tracking and intervention
2 Structured conversation with parents
3 Wider outcomes, including tackling bullying and improving attendance.

The national roll-out is being led by Sonia Blandford, under a new charity, Achievement for All (3As) Ltd, and with the support of the DfE. The charity is chaired by Brian Lamb, who was mentioned in Chapter 3 of this book in connection with the Lamb Inquiry.

Paul Green is head of one of the pilot schools. The leadership team decided to focus particularly on the third aspect of improving wider outcomes. In order to do this, the leadership team:

- created an environment of collaboration
- put strategies in place to focus on the family and to increase parental engagement
- was committed to the professional development of all staff
- had a strong vision of 'no one fails', which led to curriculum innovation.

Case study: Paul Green – Head of a pilot AfA school

The school is a small secondary school with 666 pupils on roll. It is a specialist sports college which has Trust status. It is in an area of mixed housing in a city in the Midlands. There is a wide spread of ethnic backgrounds, 36 per cent of the pupils are eligible for free school meals (FSM) and 226 pupils have been identified with SEND. The leadership team consists of the head, three deputy heads and three assistant heads. The school collaborates with five other schools in delivering the post-16 curriculum.

(Continued)

(Continued)

As part of the school's development, the staffing structure for support staff has been redefined. Teaching assistants, learning mentors, cover supervisors and family support workers, have all been replaced by a group of 20 associate teachers. Each associate teacher has a specialism, such as being a trained adviser for the Citizens Advice Bureau (CAB), a well-being adviser or a family counsellor. They each have a caseload of students and develop close working relationships with families, as well as supporting students in the classroom. They are the link between families and the other agencies working with them. Professional development for associate teachers has been made a priority, as part of raising their status and aligning their leadership structure to the teaching leadership structure.

The head teacher has been active in establishing links with outside agencies, including multi-disciplinary teams, CAMHS (the Child and Adolescent Mental Health Service), social housing and social care. Although this has been time-consuming, it has resulted in new working agreements, for instance with the Education Welfare Service (EWS) and the local Primary Care Trust (PCT). It has given the school a mechanism for meeting regularly with other professionals and having a forum to discuss with them any referrals that the school wants to put forward.

Paul and his leadership team believe that having an identified member of staff as the key worker for each family, has led to better working relationships between home and school, with parents and carers being more willing to accept support and advice. In addition, the school collaborates with external providers to sub-contract short accredited courses, such as massage, aromatherapy, nail art and meditation, which have increased the attendance, participation and achievements of a group of underachieving Year 10 girls in particular. These courses act as incentives to full participation in a more conventional core curriculum.

Further steps the school has identified include working more collaboratively with the primary schools that younger siblings attend, and trying to agree a common set of targets across all external providers.

Leading the education system

Post-war educational change has, until recently, taken a top-down approach. Michael Fullan (2004) argues that the rise in standards after the National Literacy and Numeracy Strategies (NLS and NNS) plateaued because heads did not own them. He suggests that there is something between the top-down and bottom-up approaches, which can be described as the co-production between policy makers and consumers. He argues that schools must take collective responsibility to improve the system and that sustained improvement entails heads being as concerned about improving other schools as their own.

Another example of co-production by policy makers and consumers is in the area of succession planning. This was touched on in Chapter 2, when one of the models of leadership was *sustainable leadership*.

Sustainable leadership

Successive governments have been concerned about having a sufficient supply of high quality school leaders, because of the age profile of current heads. The NCSL has encouraged schools to take seriously the idea of planning ahead in this context and to have a Succession Planning Strategy. It has put forward the idea of becoming a greenhouse school, meaning that schools should think about growing leaders from amongst their own staff.

It will have been noticed, in several of the case studies, that head teachers have found ways of extending staff's experience, by having shadow leadership teams or members of staff who rotate on the SLT in order to gain experience. This is another example of how innovate heads plan ahead, even for a future after they have moved on, because of their commitment to the long-term future of the school or schools they have helped to create.

Further reading

Department for Children, Schools and Families (DCSF) (2009a) *Achievement for All: A local authority prospectus.* Nottingham: DCSF Publications.

Fullan, M. (2004) *Systems Thinkers in Action: Moving beyond the standards plateau.* Nottingham: DfES Publications.

National College for School Leadership (NCSL) (2009b) *Greenhouse Schools: Lessons from schools that grown their own leaders.* Nottingham: NCSL.

NCSL (2011) *National Teaching Schools.* Nottingham: NCSL.

Useful websites

www.autismeducationtrust.org.uk
www.thecommunicationtrust.org.uk
www.thedyslexia-spldtrust.org.uk
www.nationalcollege.org.uk

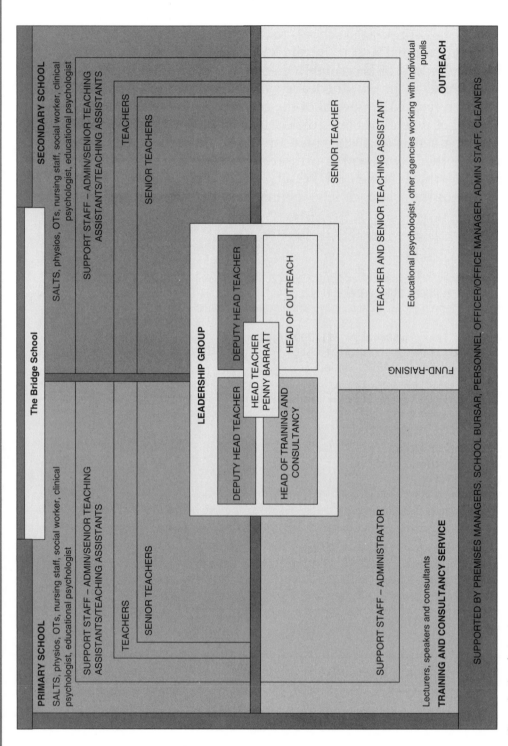

Figure 6.1 Organisational structure

The Bridge School

PRIMARY SCHOOL
SALTS, physios, OTs, nursing staff, social worker, clinical psychologist, educational psychologist

SUPPORT STAFF – ADMIN/SENIOR TEACHING ASSISTANTS/TEACHING ASSISTANTS

TEACHERS

SENIOR TEACHERS

SECONDARY SCHOOL
SALTS, physios, OTs, nursing staff, social worker, clinical psychologist, educational psychologist

SUPPORT STAFF – ADMIN/SENIOR TEACHING ASSISTANTS/TEACHING ASSISTANTS

TEACHERS

SENIOR TEACHERS

LEADERSHIP GROUP

DEPUTY HEAD TEACHER

DEPUTY HEAD TEACHER

HEAD TEACHER PENNY BARRATT

HEAD OF TRAINING AND CONSULTANCY

HEAD OF OUTREACH

FUND-RAISING

SENIOR TEACHER

TEACHER AND SENIOR TEACHING ASSISTANT

Educational psychologist, other agencies working with individual pupils

OUTREACH

SUPPORT STAFF – ADMINISTRATOR

Lecturers, speakers and consultants

TRAINING AND CONSULTANCY SERVICE

SUPPORTED BY PREMISES MANAGERS, SCHOOL BURSAR, PERSONNEL OFFICER/OFFICE MANAGER, ADMIN STAFF, CLEANERS

Photocopiable:
How Successful Schools Work © Rona Tutt and Paul Williams, 2012

Conclusion

This book has considered how the impact made by innovative leaders creates the right climate for their schools to be successful. In order to examine the effect that these leaders have, the chapters looked at different aspects of school leadership, starting with how people are attracted to becoming leaders in the first place. Each chapter has focused on one of the following questions:

- What is it about leading a school in today's climate that attracts people to become leaders?
- What models and styles of leadership do they use that encourage people to follow their lead?
- How do they manage to make all their pupils feel included when their needs, backgrounds and cultures are so different?
- How do they manage to use their power as leaders in a positive way and avoid the pitfall of misusing the power they have?
- When the pressures on them are often intense and emotionally draining, how do they manage to prioritise the well-being of staff and pupils?
- How do they keep ahead of the game in order to be innovative rather than being buffeted by changes that have been imposed on them?

Taken together, the answers to these questions help to shed light on what makes successful schools work. In a sense, it could be said that all school leaders are forced to be creative to some degree, because of the amount of change to which they must respond. However, the conversations and case studies in this book focus on those who, far from resisting the pressure of constant change, respond by looking at how it might create an opportunity to move their schools forward in different and more effective ways.

Although what is written in the sections below is set out to answer the questions already given and they reflect the order of the chapters, the information is gathered from across the book. This is because schools have become increasingly complex places with many elements to what they do. A school is not defined by whether it is an academy, a national support school, or part of a federation, as it may be all of these and many more. The schools featured in the case studies could have slotted into more than one chapter (and some are mentioned in more than one place), but a particular element of their work has been focused on, in order to cover the various aspects of school leadership and to give practical examples of how innovative leaders have approached their task.

Why people are attracted to leadership

Examples have been given of teachers who have always aimed to become heads and others who been attracted to the post because they had a clear vision for a particular school. There have been conversations with some who have come up via traditional routes and others where the Teach First and the Future Leaders programmes have attracted people with leadership qualities into the profession who might otherwise have taken a different path.

Of those who are already head teachers or principals, there are examples of heads who are attracted to stay in post by taking on fresh challenges, such as establishing a school, moving to a different school, perhaps one in difficult circumstances, or taking on additional roles. Others look for innovative ways of moving the school forward where they are, such as meeting the needs of a changing population of pupils, becoming one of the first primary academies or forming a federation. What all these heads have in common is that they are never content with what they have achieved, and part of the attraction of the role is that it puts them in the position of making the changes they think are necessary and being able to try out new ideas.

How successful leaders operate

The book has featured school leaders who are leading an assortment of successful establishments. They have contrasting personalities, but they share with each other a strong desire to make a difference, to overcome any obstacles and to be clear about the direction they want their school to take, as well as knowing how to achieve it.

They recognise the need to respond flexibly to the circumstances in which they find themselves. They are team players who are keen to put in place a more distributive style of leadership. They are happy to talk about how they have been successful and to share their knowledge, skills and experience beyond their own school. This is because they are passionate about education. Some acknowledge that running a school is becoming more like running a business, but they make it a business with a very human face.

How school leaders create an inclusive ethos

It was a very strong feature of all the school leaders that they were determined to find ways of breaking down the barriers that come between pupils and their ability to learn, or between different groups of pupils in their schools, and sometimes, between the school and the local community. As schools are a microcosm of a society that is sometimes fragmented, successful school leaders are finding innovative ways of addressing inclusion in its broadest sense. These are school leaders that make sure even very young pupils are able to contribute to the school's development, to learn about different languages and cultures and to feel that vital sense of belonging.

When the idea of schools being at the heart of their communities was first suggested, it took time for staff to adjust to the idea of working in a school that might have breakfast clubs, after-schools clubs, activities for the local community and provision on site for 0–4-year-olds, and house multi-professional teams. Today's school leaders, whatever kind of school, service or setting they lead, recognise this as an important part of their role, and one that helps them to be a catalyst for uniting communities beyond the school gates.

How those leading schools manage their power

Effective school leaders are creative people. They understand the limits of the power they have and find ways of turning the changes that are imposed on them into an opportunity to find an alternative way of leading to the one they may have planned. They are aware of the dangers that can be attached to having power, but want to share their power with others, because they know that it is the way to have a broader range of ideas and to ensure that people feel involved.

Head teachers, in particular, are aware of the strength of having a governing body that works closely alongside them and their leadership team, and will work hard to ensure that governors are people who have different areas of experience to offer. Increasingly, having sponsors or a trust, brings in additional connections and expertise.

Successful schools are led by people who have a high degree of self-awareness and who know how their actions will impact on the lives of others. They ensure that the pace of change is not unduly rapid and that there is an openness about how they work, with strong lines of communication being a priority.

How well-being is recognised as important

Effective leaders place a premium on the well-being of their staff and pupils, as well as being aware of the need to recognise the signs of stress in themselves. They are people who are resilient enough to support others and make sure that the emotional and social aspects of learning are embedded in the ethos of the school. They recognise that the well-being of staff has a knock-on effect on pupils and, consequently, on the school's results and achievements.

As a result of being innovative and delivering a creative curriculum, they make their schools exciting places to be, where pupils and their families feel involved in the process of education and there is a feeling of unity in the staffroom. Above all, they ensure that staff, pupils and their parents feel valued and respected for their contribution. Effective school leaders see their role as being, not just about personal satisfaction or advancement, but about caring passionately about the achievement of others.

How school leaders manage to be innovative

To be innovative, school leaders keep on top of the political agenda and they are adept at looking at all the opportunities that are available and deciding which ones are right for their schools at any given time. In tandem with this, they make sure their staff are involved in professional development, both through providing it to others and in updating their own professional knowledge. Offering to trial materials, or to act as a pilot school, are other ways of being part of an unfolding educational scene.

Innovative leaders understand that it is only by being aware of the political scene that they can make the right choices. While this applies to changes to legislation, to the curriculum and to the appearance of new resources (including in the rapidly changing field of technology), they are aware of opportunities that may not be flagged up as choices, but which arise from changing circumstances. For instance, there are the business opportunities which schools are likely to turn to more and more as budgets tighten and as the power of local authorities wane, in the sense of being able to offer the range of services they have done in the past. Schools offering services on their own, or in tandem with LAs or other providers, has been recognised by forward-thinking leaders as a feature of the education system that will grow in the future. Successful leaders are ones who are enterprising and able to develop new ways of working and implement new ideas.

Summarising how successful schools work

In his book, *Leadership with a Moral Purpose* (2008), Will Ryan picks out a passion for their role as the overriding personal trait shared by great school leaders. He suggests that this is tied in with having energy and self-belief, and being able to bond with like-minded people. To this, he adds the organisational trait of being strategic, which, in turn, involves having clear values, collaborating and being able to communicate a vision. Together, he suggests that these add up to performance.

Taking a slightly different slant by focusing on the culture of a school, Russell Hobby, in an investigative paper entitled *A Culture for Learning* (2004), lists the characteristics of the culture of the most successful schools as:

- having the highest ambition for every pupil
- putting the welfare of pupils ahead of the comfort of staff
- focusing on capability and learning to improve outcomes
- holding teachers to account, promoting teamwork and teachers learning from each other
- being intolerant of failure and the underperformance of staff
- valuing discipline, reliability and service delivery.

Both Ryan and Hobby pick up on some common characteristics of successful schools and the leaders who contribute to their success. Some of the points they raise appear in the list that follows, which draws out elements of the case studies and conversations outlined in this book, to compile a list of the 10 most striking characteristics shared by those who lead successful schools.

What makes successful schools work?

These characteristics appear to be similar, regardless of the size and nature of the school, the age range of its pupils or the locality in which the school is situated. Innovative leaders have much in common wherever they are working. So, in summary, successful schools are led by people who:

- thrive on change, are creative and enjoy innovating
- have a clear vision for their schools and take others with them in achieving it
- are resilient and can cope with their own stresses as well as being supportive to others
- are flexible and know how to adapt their style to different circumstances
- are passionate about improving children's life chances and are energetic in achieving this aim
- are never satisfied, but are always working on the next phase of the school's development
- appreciate the value of teamwork, have an open approach and communicate very effectively
- believe in making their schools inclusive, so that everyone is valued equally and the positive relationships between staff and pupils lead to a zest for learning
- are willing to take on additional roles, including ones that support colleagues and pupils in other schools
- enjoy keeping up to date and being at the forefront of new developments, even if there is an element of risk.

What does the future look like?

With the current pace of change, it would be a rash person who was confident about predicting the future. However, there are some pointers that would suggest the kinds of challenges school leaders will face.

The diversification of schools

It is apparent that, far from any let-up, the trend towards having a greater diversity of schools will continue. Already, the first special academies, free schools, studio schools and university technical colleges (UTCs) are appearing, to be followed by the first special free schools and alternative provision free schools. Despite this diversity, in some ways, the role of school leaders is becoming more similar as the boundaries between the phases and sectors are becoming blurred.

All-age schools are growing in number and the barriers between special and mainstream schools are being breached. Instead of being discrete entities, schools are forming chains, trusts, federations and partnerships that may go across age and phase boundaries, so schools are becoming more different and, at the same time, more like each other.

Partnerships beyond schools

The trend towards working, not just with groups of schools but with other organisations, continues. Teaching schools are another way of cementing the relationship between schools and higher education, and the growth of apprenticeships strengthens the links with the business world, as does the need for there being expertise for schools to draw on as they become more like businesses themselves.

The changing role of local authorities, as they lose personnel, combine roles and change the structure of children's services, is already seeing LAs working more closely with each other, as well as developing a new and different relationship with schools, sometimes combining to offer services in a form of co-production.

Advances in knowledge

Opportunities to deliver the curriculum in different ways will be created by continuing and accelerating changes in the technological world, with arguments to be resolved about: whether mobile and smart phones are a fantastic resource or a distraction in the classroom; how to achieve the right balance between e-books and paper-based books in classrooms and school libraries; and whether ipods and ipads have the potential to entice reluctant learners back into learning, or should be kept for time out of school. As screen-based generations begin to pass through our schools, innovative teachers will adapt how they teach and the resources they use to catch and hold pupils' interest in learning.

In addition, there are signs that neuroscientists, neuropsychologists and teachers are beginning to recognise the value of working together, in order to understand more about how children learn and how this can be translated into improving learning in the classroom for all children and young people, but especially for those with more complex needs.

Globalisation

In effect, the world will continue to shrink and schools will learn more from being aware of what is happening in other countries. School leaders and other staff will be able to share their expertise more easily and rapidly, without the need to travel, although nothing will entirely replace what is gained from visiting schools and settings in other countries.

Children and young people will become increasingly aware of being part of an international community, through many different cultures being present in most schools, towns and cities, as well as having the world literally at their fingertips.

Final thoughts

There has only been time to touch on a very few of the developments that are already occurring and are likely to lead to further changes. But one thing is clear: the pace of change will continue to increase rather than slacken and those who lead successful schools will need to be more innovative than ever, in order to keep abreast of events, to know what developments will be right for their schools, and to keep on top of the myriad of partnerships, relationships and networks that they are likely to be involved in.

In today's world, school leadership may not be for the faint hearted, but for those who have the vision, the resilience and the stamina to fulfil the role, and who do so with a passion that brings out the potential in every child who crosses their path. There is nothing as exhilarating as well as exhausting, as demanding as well as rewarding, or as vital to the future well-being of society as the job of leading schools.

References and further reading

Alexander, R. (2009) *Children, Their World, Their Education: The final report – Cambridge primary review*. London: Routledge.

Bailey, L. (2010) Building emotional resilience. *School Leadership*, 3(1): 48–51.

Baines, I. (2010) *Identify and Grow Your Own Leaders*. Nottingham: NCSL.

Bercow, J. (2008) *The Bercow Review: A review of services for young people (0–19) with speech, language and communication needs*. Nottingham: DCSF Publications.

Bullock, K. (2009) *The Importance of Emotional Intelligence to Effective School Leadership*. Nottingham: NCSL.

Bush, T. (2011) *Theories of Educational Leadership and Management*, 4th edition. London: Sage.

Bush, T., Bell, L. and Middlewood, D. (2009) *The Principles of Educational Leadership and Management*. London: Sage.

Challen, A., Noden, P., West, A. and Machin, S. (2011) *UK Resilience Programme Evaluation: Final report*. Nottingham: DfE Publications.

Clarke, G., Boorman, G. and Nind, M. (2010) 'If they don't listen I shout, and when I shout they listen': hearing the voices of girls with behavioural, emotional and social difficulties. *British Education Research Journal*, 1–16.

Davies, B. (2009) *The Essentials of School Leadership*. London: Sage.

Day, C., Harris, A., Hadfield, M., Tolley, H. and Beresford, J. (2000) *Leading Schools in Times of Change*. Buckingham: Open University Press.

Department for Children, Schools and Families (DCSF) (2007a) *Social and Emotional Aspects of Learning for Secondary Schools*. Nottingham: DCSF Publications.

DCSF (2007b) *Aiming High for Disabled Children: Better support for families*. Nottingham: DCSF Publications.

DCSF (2007c) *Planning and Developing Special Educational Provision: A guide for local authorities and other proposers*. Nottingham: DCSF Publications.

DCSF (2008) *Final Report of National CAMHs Review*. Nottingham: DCSF Publications.

DCSF (2009a) *Achievement for All: A local authority prospectus*. Nottingham: DCSF Publications.

DCSF (2009b) *The Apprenticeships, Skills, Children and Learning Act*. London: HMSO.

DCSF (2009c) *Lamb Inquiry: Special educational needs and parental confidence*. Nottingham: DCSF Publications.

DCSF (2009d) *Learning Behaviour: Lessons learned*. Nottingham: DCSF Publications.

DCSF (2010) *Salt Review: Independent review of teacher supply for pupils with severe, profound and multiple learning difficulties (SLD and PMLD)*. Nottingham: DCSF Publications.

DCSF/DoH (2008) *Children and Young People in Mind: The final report of the National CAMHS Review.* Available at www.education.gov.uk and www.dh. gov.uk

Department for Education and Science (DES) (1963) *The Newsome Report: Half our future.* London: HMSO.

DES (1967) *Plowden Report: Children and their primary schools.* London: HMSO.

DES (1970) *The Education (Handicapped Children) Act.* London: HMSO.

DES (1978) *The Warnock Report: Special educational needs.* London: HMSO.

DES (1985) *The Swann Report: Education for all.* London: HMSO.

DES (1988) *The Education Reform Act 1988.* London: HMSO.

DES (1989) *The Elton Report: Discipline in school.* London: HMSO.

DES (1992) *Curriculum Organisation and Classroom Practice in Primary Schools: A discussion paper.* London: HMSO.

Department for Education (DfE) (2010a) *The Academies Act.* London: HMSO.

DfE (2010b) *The Equality Act.* London: HMSO.

DfE (2010c) *The Importance of Teaching.* Available at: www.tsoshop.co.uk

DfE (2011a) *Support and Aspiration: A new approach to special educational needs and disability.* Nottingham: DfE Publications.

DfE (2011b) *UK Resilience Programme Evaluation: Final report.* Available at: www. education.gov.uk/publications

DfE (2011c) *The Education Act 2011.* Available at: www.legislation.gov.uk

Department for Education and Skills (DfES) (1994) *SEN Code of Practice.* Nottingham: DfES Publications.

DfES (2001) *Revised SEN Code of Practice.* Nottingham: DfES Publications.

DfES (2002) *The Education Act.* London: HMSO.

DfES (2003) *Every Child Matters:* Norwich: The Stationery Office.

DfES (2004a) *The Children Act.* London: HMSO.

DfES (2004b) *Removing Barriers to Achievement: The government's strategy for SEN.* Nottingham: DfES Publications.

DfES (2005) *Learning Behaviour.* Nottingham: DfES Publications.

Dittrich, W. and Tutt, R. (2008) *Educating Children with Complex Conditions: Understanding overlapping and co-existing developmental disorders.* London: Sage.

Department of Health (DoH)/DfES (2003) *Together from the Start.* Nottingham: DfES Publications.

DoH/Home Department (2003) *The Victoria Climbié Inquiry Report.* Available at: www.dh.gov.uk

Drucker, P. (2001) *The Essential Drucker: The best of sixty years of Peter Drucker's essential writings on management.* New York: Harper Books.

Fink, D. (2005) *Leadership for Mortals: Developing and sustaining leaders of learning.* London: Paul Chapman Publishing.

Fullan, M. (1991) *The New Meaning of Educational Change.* London: Cassell.

Fullan, M. (2001) *Leading in a Culture of Change.* San Francisco, CA: Jossey-Bass.

Fullan, M. (2004) *Systems Thinkers in Action: Moving beyond the standards plateau.* Nottingham: DfES Publications.

Gardner, H. (1976) *The Shattered Mind.* New York: Vintage.

Gardner, H. (1983) *Frames of Mind: The theories of multiple intelligence.* New York: New Horizons.

Goleman, D. (1996) *Emotional Intelligence: Why it can matter more than IQ*. London: Bloomsbury.

Goleman, D., Boyatzis, R. and McKee, A. (2004) *Primal Leadership: Learning to lead with emotional intelligence*. Boston, MA: Harvard Business School Press.

Hargreaves, D. (2009) *School Leadership Today*. Nottingham: NCSL.

Hargreaves, D. (2010) *Creating a Self-improving School System*. Nottingham: NCSL.

Hartle, F., Stein, J., Hobby, R. and O'Sullivan, M. (2007) *Retaining School Leaders: A guide to keeping talented teachers engaged*. Nottingham: NCSL.

Hill, R. (2008) *Achieving More Together: Adding value through partnership*. Leicester: ASCL.

Hobby, R. (2004) *A Culture for Learning*. London: Hay Group Education.

Hopkins, D. (2007) *Every School a Great School*. Buckingham: Open University Press.

Hopkins, D. and Higham, R. (2007) System leadership: mapping the context. *School Leadership and Management*, 27(2): 147–66.

House of Common Select Committee (2006) *Special Educational Needs: Third report of session 2005–06*, vols 1–3. London: HMSO.

Humphrey, N. and Squires, G. (2010) *Achievement for All Evaluation: Interim report*. Nottingham: DfE Publications.

MacBeath, J. (1999) *Schools Must Speak for Themselves*. London: Routledge.

Maslow, A. (1943) A theory of motivation. *Psychological Review*, 50(4): 370–96.

Munby, S, (2010) *NCSL News*. Nottingham: NCSL.

National Strategies (2010) *SEAL Priorities, 2009–2011*. Nottingham: DfE Publications.

National College for School Leadership (NCSL) (2009a) *School Leadership Today*. Nottingham: NCSL.

NCSL (2009b) *Greenhouse Schools: Lessons from schools that grow their own leaders*. Nottingham: NCSL.

NCSL (2011) *National Teaching Schools*. Nottingham: NCSL.

Nind, M., Boorman, G. and Clarke, G. (2011) Creating spaces to belong: listening to the voice of girls with behavioural, emotional and social difficulties through digital visual and narrative methods. *International Journal of Inclusive Education*, 1–14.

Ofsted (2010a) *Developing Leadership: National support schools*. Manchester: Ofsted Publications.

Ofsted (2010b) *The Special Educational Needs and Disability Review: A statement is not enough*. Manchester: Ofsted Publications.

PricewaterhouseCoopers (2007) *Independent Study into School Leadership*. Nottingham: DfES Publications.

Rose, J. (2006) *Independent Review of the Primary Curriculum: Final report*. Nottingham: DCSF Publications.

Ryan, W. (2008) *Leadership with a Moral Purpose: Turning your school inside out*. Carmarthen: Crown House Publishing.

Smith, A. with Jones, J. and Reid, J. (2010) *Winning the H Factor: The secrets of happy schools*. London: Continuum.

Stoll, L. and Fink, D. (1996) *Changing our Schools*. Buckingham: Open University Press.

Training Development Agency (TDA) (2011) *Graduate Teacher Programme.* Nottingham: DfE Publications.

Tutt, R. (2007) *Every Child Included.* London: Sage.

Tutt, R. (2010) *Partnership Working to Support Children with Special Educational Needs and Disabilities.* London: Sage.

Ward, H. (2010) Primary pioneers power next phase of academy crusade. *Times Educational Supplement*, 24 September, pp. 24–5.

Wolfe, A. (2011) *Review of Vocational Education: The Wolfe report.* Nottingham: DfE Publications.

Index

EVERY CHILD INCLUDED

Rona Tutt *Consultant, writer, researcher and former President of NAHT*

`This is an extremely timely book, which would be a very useful addition to any staffroom library' – *Special*

`One of the most detailed overviews on what is really happening with inclusion at ground level. In years to come, professionals will remember they used Rona Tutt's book for identifying where good practice was really happening. Along with Rita Cheminais and Anne Hayward, this must rate as one of the most useful texts of the decade' – *Tricia Barthorpe, Past President of the National Association of Special Educational Needs, (NASEN)*

How can your school or setting become part of a truly inclusive education service that provides for all children and young people?

Looking at the Every Child Matters agenda and the government's strategy for special educational needs (SEN), this book moves beyond the debate about specialist provision to explore the exciting developments that are taking place in both mainstream and special schools, as they join forces to provide for pupils with increasingly complex needs.

It provides examples of innovative ways forward that will help all schools develop their own strategies to support those pupils who find it hardest to learn.

Topics covered include:

- successful strategies for supporting pupils in mainstream schools
- the benefits of co-located schools, federations and partnerships
- the developing role of day and residential special schools
- the changing nature of support and advisory services

The book is essential reading for school leaders and senior management teams, and will be of interest to governors, policy makers and all those involved in the training and professional development of the school workforce.

2007 • 144 pages
Cloth (978-1-4129-4488-5) • £71.00
Paper (978-1-4129-4489-2) • £22.99
Electronic (978-1-84860-610-4) • £22.99

ALSO FROM SAGE

EDUCATING CHILDREN WITH COMPLEX CONDITIONS

Understanding Overlapping & Co-existing Developmental Disorders

Winand H Dittrich *School of Psychology, University of Hertfordshire* and **Rona Tutt** *Consultant, writer, researcher and former President of NAHT*

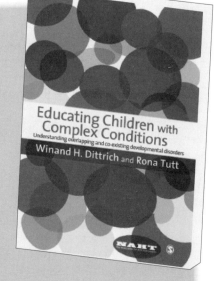

'This is an important contribution to the field of SEN. By putting the child into a context, the authors recognize that each child is unique and cannot be reduced to a simple diagnosis. Highly recommended' – *SEN Magazine*

There are growing numbers of children displaying the symptoms of more than one condition or disorder, and this has led to those involved in education needing to understand which conditions commonly overlap or co-exist, and how to meet children's more complex needs.

By bringing together some of the latest research on how the brain works with what is known about identifying developmental disorders that appear to have a common biological basis, this book looks at:

- a common group of disorders: ADHD; ASD; SLI; SpLD (including dyslexia, dyscalculia, dyspraxia and dysgraphia)
- which teaching approaches and strategies might most be relevant
- the advantages and disadvantages of labelling children

Written in a non-technical style, the book blends together scientific knowledge from different disciplines and translates it into practical terms for school leaders, practitioners in the field of special educational needs and disabilities, and students following courses in higher education.

2008 • 128 pages
Cloth (978-1-84787-317-0) • £72.00
Paper (978-1-84787-318-7) • £23.99
Electronic (978-1-84920-840-6) • £23.99

ALSO FROM SAGE

PARTNERSHIP WORKING TO SUPPORT SPECIAL EDUCATIONAL NEEDS & DISABILITIES

Rona Tutt *Consultant, writer, researcher and former President of NAHT*

In order to achieve the best outcomes for all children and young people, schools must work in partnership with students, parents, other professionals and the wider community. In this changing landscape of education, the notion of the traditional school is fast disappearing. This book looks at what is possible in this exciting new world, and how some teachers and other professionals are putting into practice the best principles of multi-agency working. It examines how partnership working affects children with SEND by considering:

- the diversity of additional needs
- the role of specialist schools that have an SEN specialism
- partnership working between mainstream and special schools
- partnership working with groups of schools, including those that are co-located or federated
- the growth of academies and trust schools
- schools and other services working together
- the work of extended schools and children's centres
- a wide range of other services for children, young people and families

Filled with case studies of effective practice from real schools and services, this book is a must-have for those looking at how to work together to achieve positive outcomes for all.

2010 • 144 pages
Cloth (978-0-85702-147-2) • £63.00
Paper (978-0-85702-148-9) • £20.99
Electronic (978-1-4462-4806-5) • £20.99

ALSO FROM SAGE